ŽIŽEK: A GUIDE FOR

Continuum *Guides for the Perplexed*

Continuum's Guides for the Perplexed are clear, concise and accessible introductions to thinkers, writers and subjects that students and readers can find especially challenging. Concentrating specifically on what it is that makes the subject difficult to grasp, these books explain and explore key themes and ideas, guiding the reader towards a thorough understanding of demanding material.

ŽIŽEK: A GUIDE FOR THE PERPLEXED

SEÁN SHEEHAN

continuum

Continuum International Publishing Group
The Tower Building   80 Maiden Lane
11 York Road   Suite 704
London SE1 7NX   New York NY 10038

www.continuumbooks.com

British Library Cataloguing-in-Publication Data
A catalogue record for this book is available from the British Library.

ISBN: 978-1-4411-8087-2 (paperback)
978-1-4411-2922-2 (hardcover)

Library of Congress Cataloging in Publication Data
Sheehan, Seán, 1951–
Žižek: a guide for the perplexed / Seán Sheehan.
   p. cm.
Includes bibliographical references (p.   ) and index.
1. Žižek, Slavoj. I. Title.
B4870.Z594S54 2011
199'.4973--dc23

2011022997

Typeset by Fakenham Prepress Solutions, Fakenham, Norfolk NR21 8NN
Printed and bound in India

CONTENTS

CHAPTER ONE

FINDING THE WAY

Studying the works of a particular writer can be imagined as a journey, the trope is a familiar one, and describing the intellectual scenery that a reader of Žižek will travel through seems a reassuring way of introducing his work. Picture books, or even ones that only use words, hold an inviting prospect; a scene that can be passively observed, a vista as the object of one's gaze, scenery to be taken in at a glance. However odd or idiosyncratic the view may appear, there will surely be some familiar-looking features and, with the provision of luminous route signs compensating for an occasional fog, the outlook should be clear enough. Alas, this is simply not the case with Žižek and the inadequacy of imagining it could be soon makes itself felt for the reader who has to engage with constantly shifting contours and negotiate a textual terrain that might charitably be described as one of excess; as orienteering aids go, a topographical map would be of more use than pictures of the landscape.

Reading some authors, especially those nurtured in academia, is like comfortably travelling on a main highway: mostly straight lines and a hierarchy of signs more or less guaranteed to take you trouble-free in linear fashion to a predetermined destination. The bending boreens and seemingly off-the-cuff detours of Žižek's writing proffer quite a different experience and it takes a while to realize that what seem like hindrances to finding one's way are in fact the gifts of the journey. The traveller invariably ends up on pathways remarkably similar to ones trod earlier, *déjà vu* becomes an occupational hazard, but repeating the route opens up scenic aspects not previously noticed, ones created in the process of return and, as well as the scree where firm footholds are missing, there are also emerging clearings where light penetrates the thickets. Sometimes, though, the topography

1

suggests an incredibly elaborate maze, relieved only by topiaries of which some are inexplicably and achingly alluring, obscurely holding out a hazy promise of something highly desirable, others clipped and trimmed into human visages with questioning gazes that discombobulate the viewer. There is an Alice in Wonderland dimension to the geography, one where results generate their own causes, where pleasure comes from the failure to reach something inaccessible and at times, when there is a sudden change of perspective, an uncanny uncertainty as to whether the landscape is the real thing or a giant simulacrum: a map of itself.

In a conventional treatise, one often expects to find at the start of a chapter a modest statement of some form of a hypothesis or a statement of intent, followed by a reference to alternative accounts by other critics or an overview of the relevant material, before the development of a new or revised interpretation by way of orderly inference and consecutive arguments. This could be labelled classical landscape writing, whereas with Žižek the established rules of perspective do not apply, for there are no rules of appearance, no vanishing point on the horizon that draws the viewer in, no background and foreground, and no fixed gaze. A chapter is likely to begin abruptly, *in medias res*, often by way of an assertive or surprising statement before spiralling away into instances designed to show that something is not what is seems to be but is almost certainly closer to being its own opposite. As landscapes go, it is as if a garden designer swept through it like a giddy Capability Brown in his wheelbarrow, mischievously placing two-way mirrors, distorting lenses and little statues of Janus where paths divide.

A difficulty is that the force of Žižek's intellectual energy can prove overwhelming and what at first is pleasantly dazzling may gradually become bewildering. By way of example, there is a part of *Did Somebody Say Totalitarianism?* that analyses the experience in Nazi concentration camps that gave rise to the 'Muslim' category of prisoner (2002b, pp. 73–88). The account begins by differentiating this category from Gulag prisoners in the Soviet era before drawing insight from the negativity that Žižek identifies in Hegel and the Lacanian Thing; it then picks up on accounts of the *gaze* of the 'Muslim' and, using examples from Greek mythology and Hitchcock's *Psycho*, shows the psychoanalytically unique nature of the 'Muslim'. Using John Ford's *The Quiet Man*, this idea is then developed to show how the 'Muslim' stands outside the genres of both tragedy and comedy and this leads back to Lacan for a now broader understanding of how the Symbolic can function as a defence against the Real, as well as a new frame for understanding the Nazi concentration camp. The account concludes by returning to the victims of Stalin's show trials, the differences and similarities with victims of Nazism.

To take another example, the first chapter of *In Defense of Lost Causes* (2009b, pp. 17–51) gets going by skirting around the nature of civility and the custom of potlatch, dips into Shakespeare's *Troilus and Cressida* before changing tack and engaging with Mel Gibson's anti-Semitism and an episode from recent Polish politics, concluding with a trenchant warning of why we should be deeply disturbed by those who accept torture as a legitimate subject for debate. The second chapter launches into film criticism, questioning what might seem like a progressive intent in films such as *Titanic*, *Reds*, *The Lives of Others*, *Goodbye Lenin* and *The Da Vinci Code*, before looking at Mary Shelley's *Frankenstein* and Kafka's letter to his father as more interesting instances of family dramas. The first part of this book draws to an end by looking at Foucault's defence of the Iranian revolution as a preliminary to a careful reading of Heidegger and his relationship with Nazism. There seems to be a compulsion to develop asides and take detours, as if laying down pieces of a scholarly jigsaw, and even critics sympathetic to Žižek cannot resist making tongue-in-cheek but tart remarks that imply a loose centre of gravity at worst – 'It is not exactly that he digresses, since there is nothing for him to digress from'[1] – or at best express a thinly disguised degree of exasperation at the vertiginous speed with which he segues from one topic to another. The range of subject areas over which Žižek finds food for his arguments is astonishingly wide – philosophy, psychoanalysis, film studies, political theory, history, current events, popular culture, literature, opera, classical music, linguistics, theology – and such a rate of consumption would be diagnosed as a serious case of intellectual obesity were it not for his accomplished mastery in these disciplines and discourses. Most readers, and this includes swathes of the academic community, are simply not used to following an author who, within a couple of pages or even less, seems to manically hop from one philosopher or psychoanalytic disquisition to another while analysing a scene from a Hollywood movie. His reasoning is experienced as too febrile for many readers' comfort levels and one way of rationalizing such discomposure is to suppose, quite mistakenly, that he may be wilfully confusing his audience or engaging in intellectual gymnastics for the sake of a theatrical display. The high-speed rate at which ideas are developed and expressed can be as disconcerting as it is exhilarating and what Adorno said of Hegel applies equally to Žižek: 'the reader has to develop an intellectual slow-motion procedure, to slow down the tempo at the cloudy places in such a way that they do not evaporate and their motion can be seen'.[2]

A Hegelian dialectic is the motor that drives Žižek's method of argumentation, allied to the Freudian insight that the repressed truth of a situation is to be found in the excess, the surplus, of what is said over and above what is consciously intended. At a very general level, what this means is that a proposition is to be investigated from wholly within itself in order to discern discrepancies that are pregnant with meaning and which lead by themselves, immanently, to an understanding that is different to the one first thought to be the case.

A QUESTION OF STYLE

That a style of writing is inseparable from what is being said – that form and content are two sides of the same coin – is obvious in the case of literary works and often not difficult to discern in philosophical texts. Wittgenstein's *Tractatus*, for example, sought to crystallize the way language relates to reality, the way names have meaning and the meaning of a name is there in the object for which it stands. Every sentence describes a state of affairs and is made up from objects, and a relationship that might happen to exist between those objects is mirrored in the grammar of a sentence, its logical syntax projecting a piece of reality; language is capable of reaching right up to reality, like a ruler laid against what it measures. The style of the *Tractatus* enacts this philosophy, refusing continuous prose and instead chooses to utter pronouncements and aphoristic statements like an oracle. The pregnant remarks constitute the work's unlikely case for the nature of language. Wittgenstein's late philosophy, enshrined in *Philosophical Investigations*, is written in a very different style and resembles a series of fragments, pieces of conversation, that reflect the way the author is no longer seduced by the idea of a binding pattern locking language and reality into a tight matrix. There is no longer a fond belief in a crystalline order: a logical essence at the heart of our language world.

Žižek's philosophy does not develop and change in the radical manner of Wittgenstein but the two philosophers share an inability to divorce what they say from their way of saying it. Underlying the sense of perplexity, that can often accompany the reading of Žižek, is a question of style and it relates to a point that he raises in his book about the films of Krzysztof Kieślowski. What makes a poem a work of poetry, he says in a footnote, is not some nugget of meaning that finds expression in the metaphoric use of language but the fact that 'a poem's "message" ... resides in the very "poetic" displacement of this meaning'.[3] Something similar, he adds, pertains to the way the unconscious desire of a dream is not to be found in the latent dream thought but in the form whereby the latent thought is displaced into the surface 'text' of the dream (this is explained at more length in the first chapter of *The Sublime Object of Ideology* (1989)). These analogies point to the way Theory can also talk about its topic as opposed to practising it: 'in philosophy, it is one thing to talk about, to report on, say, the history of subject (accompanied by all the proper bibliographical footnotes), even to supplement it with comparative critical remarks; it is quite another thing to work in theory, to elaborate the notion of "subject" itself'.[4] There is a heuretic at work in Žižek's style of writing, a resolve to write in a manner that weaves content within its form and, to borrow a metaphor he likes to use, in a way that cannot be decaffeinated. The result can be a giddying combination of exhilaration and perplexity, an addictive high-speed chase with bewildering changes in the ground that, for the reader, necessitate multiple gear shifts, sudden U-turns, three- and four-point turns, elegant loops and impossibly narrow angles to negotiate. Like the later Wittgenstein, the heuristic aspect resides in a style of writing that refuses to dominate, preferring to create patterns, provoke thought and above all avoid the possibility of having one's thought tabulated and reduced to some easily assimilable category. A small instance of this, referring to the use of a particular phrase, is made explicit in an interview given in 2007:

> Yes, but this is the problem how we use terms. I'm skeptical because the term historical materialism is for me too much identified with the core of traditional Marxism. I think a dimension which

goes beyond mere history. This more ontologically fundamental dimension of what I called death drive, negativity. Historical materialism cannot think it. It views humanity as a collective, historical subject, classes, whatever, I think we need something more and this is my style of provocation, as you probably know, to annoy my friends I sometimes consciously use this much more terrible term dialectical materialism. I like this so much because then, you know, when you use this term today, they look at you like – are you crazy? Everybody still likes the term historical materialism, it's more respectable. Dialectical materialism – it's madness. Because I like to occupy a position where, even if I am attacked and rejected, I am not contaminated, I'm very much a purist. The most important thing is not if people reject you or not but that you are not contaminated, appropriated.[5]

The avoidance of being 'appropriated' is not the result of a brazen ego insisting on a self-perceived originality; on the contrary, it brings Wittgenstein to mind once again in that the work of both these highly original thinkers is inseparable from the sense of complex personalities at play. Totally at odds with the journalistic image of Žižek, there is a high degree of cold impersonality to his work, notwithstanding a willingness to reveal a biographical or personal detail, for what really matters to him is the iteration and reiteration of arguments about the nature of being human and the ongoing need to refuse recourse to false gods – postmodernism, pluralism, multiculturalism, liberalism, tolerance, democracy – that have been enshrined on the altar of capitalism. There is, to be sure, humour in his writing, especially moribund jokes from the Soviet era, and a pleasing playfulness that finds expression in the likes of the dedication in one of his books to the *'resocialized'* dogs that used to patrol the Berlin Wall,[6] but there are no exhibitions of intimacy just as – unlike remarks made about Žižek by some commentators (and not just journalists) – there are no *ad hominem* thrusts at fellow academics. The sole criterion is always the force or relevance of an argument and because the truth is not just out there waiting to be pointed at there is no place for frivolous displays of personality. In the foreword for a series of books he edited, entitled 'Short Circuits', Žižek states his intention 'to take a major classic (text, author, notion), and read it in a short-circuiting way, through the lens of a "minor" author, text, or conceptual apparatus' in order to reveal what has become hidden or disavowed.[7]

ONTOLOGICAL IMPERATIVES

Žižek openly acknowledges and brings to the fore an aspect of existence that more usually finds expression in certain works of literature. This aspect, called the Thing by Lacan, becomes an almost unbearable, visceral horror emanating from too close a proximity to human *be-ing* and is as uncomfortable to confront within ourselves as when it is recognized in another person. Strip away the symbolic identification that confers meaning to our sense of selfhood, argues Žižek, and what remains is an utter void, a remainder and a reminder of that which was never colonized by the symbolic order of language and culture. This nothingness goes far deeper and hurts far more than what some still like to tame by calling it 'the human condition'.

From Lacan, as will be seen in the next chapter, a landscape of the soul can be drawn, a part of which correlates the emergence of human subjectivity with the Word, the name-giving command of language and the symbolic order. The signifying network constricts the body by containing it within its symbolic architecture and this is described as a mortifying process that dissociates a thing from a fuller more 'alive' context. Žižek connects this with Hegel's account of how a power of negativity in the subject breaks down and classifies the organic totality of experience into component units, treating each as if in self-sufficient possession of a positive identity. A line of shared territory between Lacan and Hegel is the profound disjunction between the symbolic world that we ordinarily inhabit and the ontological void that underpins it.

The insight that is drawn from Lacan and from German idealism is that 'reality' is not something with a positive identification in advance of and separate from the human subject. Žižek is not denying reality by saying it is all in our minds or an elaborate dream, nor ignoring the fact that there was a time in the past when humans did not exist but a world did, but he wishes to insist that the world cannot be seen as having features that exist wholly unto themselves. Reality is constituted, posited, by the subject and there is a disharmonious dynamic at work in the subject that Freud identified as the 'death drive' and which Žižek sometimes refers to as a derailment. This drive cannot be satisfied and takes a perverse pleasure, what

Lacan labelled *jouissance*, in not being satisfied. There is an affinity here with contemporary cognitive science, as with this statement by Thomas Metzinger:

> The emerging image of *Homo sapiens* is of a species whose members once longed to have immortal souls but are slowly recognising they are self-less Ego Machines. The biological imperative to live – indeed, live forever – was burned into our brains, into our emotional self-model, over the course of millennia ... Mortality is not only an objective fact but a subjective chasm, an open wound in our phenomenal self-model ... Many of us, in fact, spend our lives trying to avoid experiencing it.[8]

Žižek, in a myriad of different ways, explores an ontology premised on ideas of incompleteness and inconsistency, and the tremendous social, psychoanalytic and political implications that follow for the relationship between us as subjects and the world we live in. He reads the death drive, he states in a 2007 interview, 'not as something biological, whatever, but as an ontological, as it were, disturbance, structure which feeds to what in German idealism they call negativity'.[9]

Žižek has a love of theory and it manifests itself in a penchant for, if not an addiction to, models and theoretical constructs that can serve to represent facets of his philosophizing. The Lacanian triad of the imaginary, symbolic and real comes immediately to mind in this respect and he also likes the Greimas Square, a construct developed by the linguist Algirdas J. Greimas to represent binary relationships between semiotic signs. Most emblematic of Žižek's thought is perhaps his recourse to the twisted loop of the Moebius strip, where the following of a line down its middle brings about a change from one side to the other, thus creating only one side. Matters of interest to Žižek rarely turn out to be what their appearance first suggests and the chances are that analysis will show them to be the very opposite. This is not an aspect of an inherently whimsical style or an indulgence in paradox for its own sake, although an exasperated reader may sometimes feel this is indeed the case, but the result of an analytical method founded on linguistics, psychoanalysis and German idealism. The results of his explorations into theory are surprising and often paradoxical, as when he concludes an analysis of *The Matrix* by acknowledging what is interesting about the film – its juxtaposition of reality envisaged as a virtual order subject to alteration and the disavowed truth that this domain of freedom can render the subject passive and submissive – but points out that its ending is not realizing an emancipatory release into our true state of being but actually the very opposite:

> We are not dreaming in VR [virtual reality] that we are free agents in our everyday common reality, while we are actually passive prisoners in the prenatal fluid exploited by the matrix; it is rather that our reality is that of the free agents in the social world we know, but in order to sustain this situation, we have to supplement it with the disavowed, terrible, impending fantasy of being passive prisoners in the prenatal fluid exploited by the matrix. The mystery of the human condition, of course, is why the subject needs this obscene fantasmatic support of his existence.[10]

BACKGROUND OF AN ICONOCLAST

Some biographical information may help to provide a context for Žižek's complex intellectual personality and his iconoclasm, notwithstanding his own remark that his life is 'straightforward': 'Nothing happened. At 15, I wanted to be a movie director. But I saw some really good European films and I accepted that I couldn't do that. Then, at 17, I decided to become a philosopher.'[11]

He was born in 1949 in Ljubljana, Slovenia, the only child of parents who held professional jobs, and grew up in the wake of World War II and at a time when Slovenia was part of communist Yugoslavia. Asked in an interview if he had a happy childhood, he replied: 'No. You could say, in a vulgar Freudian way, that I am the unhappy child who escapes into books. Even as a child, I was most happy being alone. This has not changed.'[12] Some family rancour resulted from resistance to his father's wish for him to become an economist like himself and Slavoj studied philosophy instead. Yugoslavia under Tito was not as ideologically hard-lined as other Eastern-bloc countries and the young Žižek had access to Western books and films that would not have been so readily available elsewhere. Studying philosophy and sociology, he graduated from the University of Ljubljana in 1971 and began work for a thesis on French structuralism for a post-graduate qualification; there were good indications that he would gain a permanent teaching position at the university, but this was not to be the case. A change in the political climate caused his intellectual interests to be regarded with suspicion by the powers that be: 'I remember that when I finished my Master's thesis, I had to write a special supplement because the first version was rejected for not being Marxist enough![13] – and he was passed over for a university post. This was a severe disappointment and, in between paid work as a translator and time spent completing his National Service in the Yugoslav Army, he was more or less unemployed for a number of years until in 1977 he took up a position, 'a humiliating job' where he was supposed 'to vegetate on the margins', as he puts it in the film *Žižek!*, at the Central Committee of the League of Slovene Communists. Two years later, he found a post at the Department of Sociology in the Institute for Social Sciences at the University of Ljubljana. This proved pleasantly undemanding and Žižek was allowed to pursue his interests in philosophy and Lacanian psychoanalysis. Looking back at his failure to secure the university post he had expected, Žižek is upbeat:

> And this was a blessing in disguise. After a period of unemployment I got a post at an out-of-the-way university. I was able to survive and I had the freedom to develop my own ideas. Without that communist oppression I honestly believe I would be a stupid professor in Ljubljana. I am very lucky![14]

By the early 1980s his work on philosophy from a Lacanian perspective was published in Slovenia and, working with colleagues who shared this approach, he began to edit and write introductions to translations into Slovene of works by Freud and Althusser as well as fiction by G. K. Chesterton. His intellectual pursuits led to spending a year in Paris and many visits thereafter as a result of studying under Jacques-Alain Miller – Lacan's son-in-law and a highly influential Lacanian in his own right. Miller helped secure for him a teaching fellowship – this was around the time that his marriage to a fellow Slovenian came to an end – and Žižek also underwent psychoanalysis with Miller, an experience that Žižek described in an interview in such a way that it is difficult to know how much of the account is tongue-in-cheek.[15] Žižek eventually found permanent academic employment in Ljubljana, not teaching in a university but as a researcher at the Institute for Sociology. This turned out to be ideal in some respects because he was allowed to pursue his own interests without the burden of teaching. These interests now included national politics and in 1988 he was a member of a group that publicly resigned from the Communist party in protest at a political trial.[16] These were turbulent years, with the beginning of effective opposition inside Slovenia and the formation of a Committee for the Defence of Human Rights. In 1990 he stood for a seat on the four-member Slovenian collective presidency and narrowly lost election.

Žižek's first book in English, *The Sublime Object of Ideology*, appeared in 1989 and took most people in western Europe and North America by surprise because so little was known about the author, although he had already published articles and books in Slovenian and French. Like the birth of Athena, fully formed and armoured as the goddess of the intellect, Žižek seemed to have arrived out of the blue, making a stunning début with a book that secured him instant attention and respect because of the stylistically arresting way it combined ideas from Lacan with those of Hegel. More books followed in quick succession and his astonishing output of work has continued apace, displaying a tremendous knowledge of different academic fields and an encyclopaedic acquaintance with films, fiction and non-fiction and various aspects of popular culture.

In the film *Žižek!* he says the four of his books that are most dear to him are *The Sublime Object of Ideology* (but with some reservations), *For They Know Not What They Do*, *The Ticklish Subject* and *The Parallax View* but readers have many more from which they can make their own choice of favourites. Žižek's ability to hold an audience is legendary (and the source of much hyperbole on the part of journalists) and his tremendous success as a speaker has helped make him a visiting professor at universities in the USA and the holder of university posts in Ljubljana and London; he continues to live in Slovenia but appears all around the world in symposiums.[17] One consequence of his fame as a public intellectual has been the opportunity to express his views on current social and political events, and over recent years it has not been uncommon to find his views in newspapers such as the *Guardian* and the *New York Times*, and interviews on major television networks like Al Jazeera and the BBC. These are nearly always sober in tone and content but occasionally, as in an interview for the *Guardian* in 2008, his witty replies bear witness to the iconoclasm that is such a defining feature of his work.[18]

CHAPTER TWO

LACAN AND ŽIŽEK

The terms that follow come from Lacan's work and while allowance is given for some of the ways in which Žižek construes Lacanian ideas there is little testimony to the changes and developments in Lacan's own use and understanding of his key terms nor to the ambiguity and complexity that, over the course of his teaching, he brought to bear on his own thought.

THE IMAGINARY

There is a stage in the infant's life that Lacan called the mirror stage. The infant's body, in the throes of a profound alienation as it struggles to master its fragmented and uncoordinated self, forms a pleasurable identification with an image that, like a reflection in a mirror, offers a sense of recognition and self-belonging, a sense of self. The comfort of a unified wholeness within oneself is identified with an image – the face of the mother, for example, or a reflection in a real mirror – and this becomes the basis for the formation of the ego. Importantly, though, this is an act of mis-recognition because the sense of wholeness is identified with something outside of oneself – an object, a *'petit autre'* or small other – the result of a placement in an image and not within oneself. In this way, the process of constituting oneself involves what Lacan called the imaginary – a term associating the sense of 'imagined' – not really there – with that of the image as a visual presence. This process of constituting oneself is inseparable from the formation of the ego and from a disavowal of the lack of a whole being-ness. It is this lack of full ipseity that gives rise to the imaginary in the first place and to the illusory import of the unity lying behind the formation of the ego.

The imaginary has a specular and narcissistic basis but in a child's development it intertwines with immersion into the world of language and this brings another register, that of the symbolic, into Lacan's philosophical anthropology.

THE SYMBOLIC

Language as the primary symbolic medium though which we interpret the world is a familiar idea and it can be taken as a given background for Lacan's concern with the consequences of being born into and socialized within a symbolic order. The signifier is arbitrary and there is no position outside of language that allows us to compare words and things, to see how language hooks on to reality; there is no escape from its closed synchrony so that while a proposition like 'there is a table in the room next door' can be compared with the existing state of affairs and its accuracy judged 'such a procedure already relies on the language-totality for the very meaning of the proposition "There is a table in the room next door"'.[1] This aspect of the symbolic, worth stressing because of the way it is taken up by Žižek, is the idea that language preserves what it refers to and defies nature (where everything dies) by bestowing a permanence upon the transient. Words as symbols can endow what is signified with a life after death, overcoming what is empirically present by the power of nomination. This is a form of immortality but also one of mortification: 'For a human being to be "dead while alive" is to be colonized by the "dead" symbolic order'.[2]

The register of the symbolic is a complex network of linguistic and cultural signs, a chain of signification that makes sense of the world and our position within it. The chain is not just a series of links, with one signifier depending on another (like a dictionary, premised on differences yet explaining one word by using another one), but is also a containment that defines where a person stands within the symbolic order. The symbolic order operates in language and for Lacan the subject can be seen in an important respect as an effect of language rather than its cause. The anteriority of the symbolic means that we are *subjected* to it in two senses: first, born into it, we are obliged, coerced, to acquire through language our sense of who we are; second, we are given our very subjecthood in this way. It is language and the symbolic order more generally that bestows subjecthood upon us and Lacan refers to the subject of the enunciated, meaning by this term the subject that is spoken through and inscribed by language.

The transition from the imaginary to the symbolic is bound up with the child's negotiation of feelings towards its mother and other family members and for Lacan, following Freud, this crucial stage of development is fraught with complex issues that he explores through terms that include the Other and Name of the Father.

THE OTHER

The Other is different from and outside of oneself and there is a radicality to the alterity of this experience that earns the term its capitalization. The little, non-capitalized other is the other person as a reflection of one's own ego, a projection of the imaginary order, my ideal Ego. The Other cannot be assimilated in this way.

The mother provides an anchorage for the infant's construction of an imaginary consistency but also a rude awakening and the earliest experience of an insufficiency comes when the child is forced to acknowledge that the mother's love is not total. The mother becomes the first Other in the infant's world and the (m)Other who feeds and nurtures, imagined to fulfil every demand and desire, is found to have desires of her own, ones which are not fulfilled by the infant. This inaugural encounter with the inscrutability of the Other's desires establishes an experience that is repeated throughout life and it is the meaning of Lacan's *Che vuoi?* ('what do you want?'): what does the Other want? It is a part of what constitutes freedom:

> In this difficult predicament, full of anxiety, when I know *that* the Other wants something from me, without knowing *what* this desire is, I am thrown back into myself, compelled to assume the risk of freely determining the coordinates of my desire.[3]

The infant, though, continuing to be nurtured as before and with its creaturely needs being met, has a longing for a complete and undivided love which is not fulfilled. The symbolic order accompanies the Other and with Otherness comes the Oedipus complex and the Name of the Father.

THE NAME OF THE FATHER

The Oedipus complex has a notoriety that clouds its basic value as a way of referring to the ambivalent feelings that develop between a child and its earliest experience of the Other. The child, discovering that there is another object of the mother's desire, is forced to asked a question: What and where am I in relation to the desire of the Other? This is the source of the traumatic awareness of an intrusion into the imaginary state of a blissful symbiosis with the (m)Other – what am I if I cannot meet all the (m)Other's demands? – and the 'father' is a solution to this enigma. What is important here is that the figure of the father is not the source of the intrusion, not the actual deadlock which introduces a breach in desire, but a means of symbolizing, and thereby allaying, the angst of having to confront the insufficiency of myself. The Name of the Father is Lacan's term for the symbolic position, outside of oneself, occupied by the object of the mother's desire. Before this position is localized, the object of the mother's desire, that which was evoked to explain the mother's periodic withdrawals, is a mystery. Now, the figure of the father provides 'a compromise solution that alleviates the unbearable anxiety of directly confronting the Void of the Other's desire'.[4]

The Name of the Father should not be reduced to an actual father – there may not be a male in the young child's life – but the figure represents entry into the authority of the symbolic, the law, the breaking of the imaginary bond of plenitude between child and mother by the surgical cut of the signifier.

Entry into the symbolic brings a symbolic identity for the child and thereby a gap is created between this identity and the subjective awareness of a personal identification with the mother. Lacan's term for this is 'symbolic castration' and the phallus becomes the signifier, the insignia, for the assumed symbolic identity and the sense of loss that this creates. 'The phallic signifier is, so to speak, an index of its own impossibility.'[5] It is for this reason that Lacan calls the square root of -1 the 'imaginary' number that is the 'meaning' of phallus.[6] The square root in question is not a number that ordinarily exists, although there are good reasons why mathematicians want to be able to represent it; similarly, the phallus represents the impossible fullness that cannot exist but which still functions at the level of meaning. The phallus is imaginary because it takes the place of and represents the object of the mother's desire; its potency is imaginary although the child has to submit to the Name of the Father as the possessor of the phallus. In the way that it represents the fact that the mother–child dyad has been broken, that the Other is not purely the mother but lies elsewhere, the phallus is also symbolic. It is figurative and while not to be equated with the physical male organ it can, because of the way it signifies the mask of a symbolic identity, be seen as 'a kind of organ without a body which I put on, which gets attached to my body, but never becomes an organic part, forever sticking out as its incoherent, excessive prosthesis'.[7] The hysteric, for Lacan and for Žižek, is someone who questions their symbolic mask, and Lacan identifies woman with phallus because they share the fact 'that their being is reduced to a pure semblance. In so far as femininity is a masquerade, it stands for phallus as the ultimate semblance'.[8]

THE BIG OTHER

The Name of the Father is part of the child's early experience of the Other, but entry into the symbolic involves a whole Other network, and the Lacanian term for the broad symbolic field into which we are born and from where we acquire recognition as a subject is the big Other. It can be equated with the matrix in the film *The Matrix*: 'the virtual symbolic order, the network that structures reality for us'.[9] This capitalized big Other is not necessarily an individual as such, although in a particular situation one person may take on the role of the big Other. More generally, the big Other is the fabric of socially defined knowledge and the set of rules governing our behaviour and speech. To fall out of this network, to cease to believe in its efficacy, is to be rendered, in psychoanalytic terms, a psychotic.[10]

When the term is used to refer generally to the set of collectively held beliefs that underlie a particular social field, it is the fictional quality of the big Other that merits Žižek's attention. The big Other does not always know everything but it is supposed to and, because it normalizes intersubjective space, any perceived breakdown in the functioning of the big Other can induce anxiety. Satisfaction comes from being the object of the Other's gaze, it serves to validate one's existence, and Žižek finds instances of this in the Romans' habit of placing sculptures high up on aqueducts where they could hardly be seen from the ground or the television success of 'Big Brother' programmes.[11]

Žižek draws a conceptual parallel between the nature of Lacan's big Other and a 'form-of life' as described by Wittgenstein.[12] Participation in both is mediated by language and the act of speaking is a form of pact between those taking part. It could not make sense to ask what premises and presuppositions are held by participants because such an order of questioning is not allowed for in the a priori set of attitudes and values that go to make up certainty. This is not a question of truth in that truth is not part of the hermeneutic equation governing a form of life. Certainty is ungrounded and its framework does not allow this groundlessness to be contemplated; its axioms cannot be questioned. Beyond a certain point, there is no position for sanctioning a further level of questioning. A form of life, like the big Other, is not equivalent to truth; it closes down the possibility of doubt but without any positive fact to substantiate this act of closure. This lack reveals the shifting foundations on which it is built and this is one way of understanding what Lacan means by saying 'there is no big Other'.[13] It does not literally mean that the big Other does not exist but that it lacks consistency, self-identity and internal cohesion.

The big Other functions ordinarily as a regulatory force providing the subject with a consistent sense of his or her identity. Any mutation in this 'natural' face of the big Other signals a disruption to the subject's impression of normality and Žižek maps out just such a development by contrasting the role of the Other in Hitchcock with that of *film noir*. In a typical scene from a Hitchcock movie, like the auction in *North by Northwest*, the hero uses the unawareness of the public to escape from his pursuers. In a *noir* film such innocent ignorance on the part of the Other, the neutrality of the big Other, is compromised and the customary frame of intersubjective reference, destabilized by suspicion and double-cross, becomes part of the existential threat to the hero. This dislocation is cinematically rendered by the visual displacements that characterize *film noir* (the eccentric camera angles, disturbances in the play of light and shade), an undermining of conventional art's framing devices that brings the paintings of Hopper into the *noir* universe.[14]

A question that has not been addressed so far is, if the subject's sense of identity is bound up with the functioning of the big Other, can a process of subtraction leave us with some notion of an authentic subject?

THE SUBJECT

The subject is not to be found in the ego, which belongs to the realm of the imaginary. The ego is formed by a series of identifications with things outside of itself and the finding there of emblems for that full being-ness that is lacking. The much-used metaphor of peeling an onion, removing one layer after another only to finally reveal nothing, captures the sense of the ego's layered composition and the emptiness, the void, that remains were these layers to be removed. The ego, by providing a fictitious wholeness, serves as a protective formation against this void; an onion looks as if it might reveal something substantial after being peeled.

Is it, then, in the symbolic order that the subject develops and expresses itself? Mention has been made of the subject of the enunciated but this is the subject positioned within and by the symbolic network, governed by the big Other. Here too there is a lack of being because the subject inscribed by the symbolic order is spoken by it; there is no signifier which would be the subject's 'own' and thus no position where the subject can locate itself. Another way of approaching this is to think of the lack that is inherent in language: if everything needed was simply there then language would be superfluous. There is an inherent insufficiency and instability to the subject despite the apparent permanence and self-identity that attaches itself to the 'I' in language. Lacan's terms for this speaking 'I' is the subject of the enunciation (as opposed to the subject of the enunciated) but this 'I', the non-substantial barred subject, is a 'logical variable'[15] and can come from different sources. Žižek likes the example of the accused in Stalinist show trials who confesses to being a traitor (the subject of the enunciated) because he has been convinced that as a good Communist (as the subject of enunciation) this is the best thing to do.[16]

Lacan represents the subject as $, with the bar representing its entry into language and the lack of a signifier to adequately represent it. The subject is empty in that it embodies a lack and the bar in $ indicates also that it is split – between the self of the ego and the failure of the symbolic to properly represent it. In Žižek's words: 'The intimate link between *subject* and *failure* lies not in the fact that "external" material social rituals and/or practices forever fail to reach the subject's innermost kernel, to represent it adequately ... but on the contrary, in the fact that the "subject" itself is *nothing but* the failure of symbolization, of its own symbolic representation.'[17] Philosophers may ask why is there something rather than nothing, but for the subject the question is why is there nothing when there should be something.[18]

At this stage it is important to stress that it does not follow that the very notion of a subject is itself a hollow fiction. Loss is constitutive of subjectivity and the effect of the gap between me and my symbolic identity is the subject and in this way, founded on lack, 'the subject "is" the very gap filled in by the gesture of subjectivization'.[19] But, at the same time, there is a subject prior to subjectivization, even though this subject is not part of an ontological order that gives it the substance of its being. How this can be and how Žižek can salvage from it the subject as something positive and meaningful will be examined later.

The subject as the embodiment of a lack is clearly an alienated, decentred subject but this does not mean that if only the cause of alienation could be overcome then the true self would reveal itself and find authentic expression. There is no 'true' self because the self is the vacant medium for a set of imaginary and symbolic identifications and thus the split in the subject referred to above is *the division between something and nothing*.[20] The point is that the subject's lack is constitutive, this lack of being *is* the subject of the symbolic. This lack is also constitutive of desire.

DESIRE

As Žižek explains: 'every time the subject gets the object he demanded, he undergoes the experience of "This is not *that*!"'Although the subject "got what he asked for," the demand is not fully satisfied. since its true aim was the Other's love, not the object as such, in its immediate particularity.'[21] The Other's love would be recognition of the subject but what the subject experiences is the enigma of its own desire – a puzzling lack of gratification that raises the question of what is it that is being desired – *and* the enigma of what is it that the Other desires. In Lacan's words:

A lack is encountered by the subject in the Other, in the very intimation that the Other makes to him by his discourse ... there emerges in the experience of the child something that is radically mappable, namely, *He is saying this to me, but what does he want?*[22]

This *Che vuoi?* is addressed to the Other, asking what is there in me that goes beyond my symbolic identity, but also a self-address arising from the mystery of the subject's existence. It leads to the subject desiring through the desire of the other, wanting to be whatever it is that accounts for the awareness of a lack in the Other.

There is a need and there is something that is demanded and, as Lacan puts it, desire is what is left when the one is subtracted from the other:

> Thus desire is neither the appetite for satisfaction, nor the demand for love, but the difference that results from the subtraction of the first from the second, the phenomenon of their splitting (*Spaltung*).[23]

This remainder, a 'beyond' that is not embodied in physical demands like those for food or drink or expressible in the language which articulates such demands, is what constitutes the unassuageable force of desire. This force cannot be satisfied – the unmediated everything that the infant looks to the mother for is not there – and it is the lack of satisfaction that sustains desire. Without the lack there would be no desire and it is the searching, not the finding, that lies at the heart of desire. Self-fuelled by endless deferrals, the paradox is that anxiety may be caused not by an endless searching but by the possibility of getting too close to the object of our search and thereby losing desire.

Desire is often associated with transgression because of the way ethical moderation is seen to involve an avoidance of extremes and the control of desires which may always run amok. A further aspect of the paradox of desire is that the miser, whose obsession is the excessive attachment to the moderate virtue of prudence, becomes for Žižek the exemplary example of desire's perverse logic: '[he] invests moderation itself with desire (and thus with a quality of excess): don't spend, economize: retain instead of letting go ... And it is only *this* desire, the very anti-desire, that is desire *par excellence*'.[24]

Desire desires desire.[25] It is the lack which constitutes desire, the lack that is in the Other as a desiring subject, the lack that could be filled by desiring through the Other's desire. This is what sustains the *objet petit a*.

OBJET PETIT A

Lacan endows *objet petit a* (little object a) with a Janus-like identity by referring to it as the 'object-cause' of desire': 'the chimerical object of fantasy, the object causing our desire and at the same time – this is its paradox – posed retroactively by this desire'.[26] It is this puzzle – how can something be both the object of desire and yet the cause of that desire in the first place? – that lies behind its complex but revealing nature.

The barred subject, as seen, is Lacan's term for representing the lack in an individual's sense of identity. There is an ontological void at the core of our subjectivity and it is this incompleteness that *objet petit a* masks and compensates for, but only seemingly so – the impression of completeness in one's identity that *objet petit a* provides is delusory. It is a fantasy object that fills out the fissure in our sense of being, arising from the way our libidinal investment gives it a sublimity that it does not and cannot possess. An abiding attractiveness is attached to the object because it represents something that is felt to have been lost and which will bring closure if only it can be found. It is a fantasy object not because it does not exist but because it does not have the quality attributed to it. It does not represent the discovery of something lost, for such an object never existed in the first place; through fantasy it holds out the possibility of embodying that indefinable, rapturous something that is experienced as missing in our lives. By enshrining what is felt to be missing, loss becomes possible but this is an autobiographical falsehood because the loss is presupposed. Lacan's example for this paradoxical object is the lady of the knight's Sisyphean quest in courtly love; always unattainable, the lady has no confirmed identity but serves purely to map the space of desire – why? – because 'the *objet a* is not a positive entity existing in space, it is ultimately nothing but a certain *curvature of the space itself* which causes us to make a bend precisely when we want to get directly at the object'.[27] The metaphor of curved space is for Žižek a way of marking the difference between the object and the cause of desire: 'no matter how close I get to the object of desire, its cause remains at a distance, totally elusive'.[28] The little object a is a placebo that enables desire to desire: 'it is this object which keeps the gap of desire open'.[29]

For Lacan, this relationship between the divided subject and the object invested with a sublimity is so bound up with the nature and

function of fantasy that it becomes his formula for fantasy: $ ◊ a
($ as the barred subject, a as *objet petit a* and the lozenge symbol
formalizing their interaction).

Looking at the term more formally, in terms of structure, it has
been seen how there is a lack in the symbolic order, a point which is
empty because the symbolic order is constitutively unable to make
good the deficit. This default has to be set right by something,
anything, that can assuage the subject's sense of loss. An object can
be drawn in for this purpose and thereby invested with the force
of desire. In this way it is given a consistency and fixity it does not
possess. There is a contingency at work and yet it seems like a process
of recovery, as if the object is what we were always seeking and now
finally is recoverable. In truth, this way of seeing it only arises *after*
the object has been positioned in the way it has; it is a retroactive
positing, the object only coming to have a sublime quality after
its association with the gap that it seems to fill: '*the place logically
precedes objects which occupy it*'.[30]

The object that is retroactively posited is what sets desire in
motion by embodying the 'beyond' that cannot be satisfied by merely
meeting the child's physical needs. The object is said to be invested
with a force of desire but this force is only brought into play by the
movement that postulates a particular object as being able to fill
the void in our sense of being. Desire is desire for a whole love, a
completeness, a density of being that does not exist and it is only
when an object is retroactively posited as being the goal of our desire
that desire is realized in a concrete form; it is in this sense that *objet
petit a* is both the object and cause of desire.[31] Part of the difficulty
in understanding this paradoxical identity of the object resides in
grasping its retroactive positioning. There is a dormant desire to fill
the void that haunts subjectivity and without this there would be no
possibility of an object able to embody this lack but the object only
becomes something rather than nothing when it is so posited. The
posited object creates desire by giving a positivity to the lack, in the
same way that the failure of the symbolic to provide a representation
for the subject becomes the positive condition for the fundamental
lack that is the subject itself.

There is another aspect to the infant's relationship with the
Other that feeds into the nature of *objet petit a*. With the acknowledgement of the Other as another barred subject with its own lack,
the interaction between the two gives rise to the dilemma of trying to

answer the question 'where am I positioned in relation to the Other's desire?' A distance is established that differentiates the desire of the subject from the desire of the Other, but although this distance is an insuperable one there always remains a something that can sustain the desire that the infant once thought was achievable with the mother. This something, this remainder, takes the form of the irrecuperable *objet petit a.*

There is something ineluctable about the object-cause of desire but reaching the ultimate satisfaction that is held out as the prize of attainment is impossible. In the Lacanian formula for fantasy, $ \$ \lozenge a $, this impossibility is part of the interaction represented by the lozenge symbol and Žižek finds his own representation for this in Zeno's paradox of Achilles and the tortoise: 'the topology of this paradox of Zeno is the paradoxical topology of the object of desire that eludes our grasp no matter what we do to attain it'.[32] *Objet petit a* is inseparable from the feeling of loss and metaphysical pain that gives rise to it but is equally inseparable from the pleasure that accompanies its sought-for presence in our life. The result is enjoyment plus pain: 'like the castrato's voice, the *objet petit a* – the surplus enjoyment – arises at the very place of castration'.[33]

DRIVE

Drive in Freud is usually but misleadingly translated as instinct, denoting a purely primitive, biological urge rather than pointing towards the concept of a force linking a demand of the body with an imposition on the psyche. An instinct can be satisfied, like the body's instinctive need for food, but a drive cannot be contented. Žižek makes this point by differentiating the goal of a drive (which in the case of the oral drive could be eliminating hunger) from its aim (the satisfaction of chewing, sucking swallowing).[34]

Desire and drive are related terms in Lacan, but while they overlap they are not synonymous. To move from desire to drive involves a shift from the lost object, posited as that which would make good the sense of loss, to loss itself as the object; in this sense, desire is a manifestation of drive. There is a gap in the symbolic because of the rupture in the order of being that the symbolic itself is witness to. The symbolic cannot symbolize itself, cannot step outside its frame and represent what is beyond its own powers of representation, and drive circulates directly around this gap in the ecology of being. This is not the same as desire fastening on an object that is invested with the force, the sense of loss, that comes from the emptiness that is the hole.[35]

This difference between desire and drive accounts for the way *objet petit a* functions, equivocally, on two levels. As the object of desire, *objet petit a* emerges as the lost object but this object is not to be found, it does not exist, and the drive is impelled to press on, driven by its hopelessness to try and circumvent the impasse. With the prospect of a route to the lost object closed irrevocably, driving forward is the only possibility and, in this its second level, *objet petit a* is also the object of drive. This time it is loss itself and not some particular object that is *objet petit a*: 'the weird movement called "drive" is not driven by the "impossible" quest for the lost object; it is *a push to directly enact the "loss" – the gap, cut, distance – itself*'.[36] Drive resides in the human condition and the distinction between instinct and drive is one way of representing the development from the animal to the human dimension. Unlike humans, animals are not subjected to an instinct that fixates itself on an activity which then becomes a self-satisfying end in itself.[37]

Desire is transferable – any object has the metonymic ability to stand in for the void – but drive, compelled to fixate on loss itself, is inert. This distinction helps understand the Lacanian view of the death drive but before looking at this term it helps to bring into the picture something that has been an unspoken background to much of what has been introduced up to now. This something, another order of experience, is the Real.

THE REAL

The Lacanian Real, often but not always capitalized, is a slippery idea to firmly grasp and in the course of reading Žižek the difficulty of such a task is likely to increase at times. Important aspects of Žižek's thought develop through his continuing engagement with the nature of the Real and the concept serves as his compass but with the needle sometimes hovering as if it wants to point in different directions at the same time. This is not the result of an error in intellectual orientation but something that arises immanently, a necessary ambivalence that attaches itself to the nature of the Real. Žižek is less charitable towards himself and admits to the need for a revised account of the term; a development that is partially signalled in what follows by referring sometimes to an 'early' Žižek, as opposed to his later, recalibrated accounts of the Real.

A very obvious difficulty with the Real is that it refers to something unrepresentable; something that manifests itself but not within the symbolic matrix. This encourages thinking of the Real as the primordial level of naked, amorphous materiality, that which is 'really' there, unprocessed, underneath or behind the symbolic patterning which accounts for the matrix of representations that we call reality. Sometimes, as when Žižek alludes to the restaurant scene in Terry Gilliam's *Brazil* featuring the difference between the photo of a meal and the slime that sits on the plate brought by the waiter, this is the distinction he might be thought to be making.[38] When he says that ordinary reality is like a beautiful naked body and the Real is the palpitating mélange of glands, tissue and veins that we can envision, with revulsion and fascination, existing beneath the thin surface of the skin, or that what Freud sees when he looks into the throat of his patient, in his famous inaugural dream of Irma's injection, is this Real, Žižek's examples might seem to reinforce this interpretation.[39]

This way of looking at the Real, as something occludent but always there, is present in early Žižek and can be discerned in his reference to a moment from Robert Heinlein's science fiction story *The Unpleasant Profession of Jonathan Hoag* when a lowered car window reveals a grey mistiness inchoately making its presence felt and seeping inside the car; what else is this, Žižek rhetorically asks, if not the Lacanian Real: 'the pulsing of the presymbolic substance in its abhorrent vitality'.[40] The Real exists in the interstice that the windowpane gives form to; it is there waiting to irrupt. Whatever Heinlein may have meant by what was on the other side of the windowpane, Žižek's understanding of it should be taken at the metaphorical level and it needs stressing that when he evokes a scene such as this, or the one from *Brazil*, or when the surface/depth difference in the appearance of a body is alluded to, he is *not* delineating the Real as the ultimate source of reference for reality.[41] It is because there is no such ultimate reference that, in later Žižek, the Real is the change in perspective that produces a different way of looking at and experiencing reality. This is not to be taken as a form of relativism, as can be seen from his example from Hitchcock's *Vertigo* and the way Judy, who earlier in the story was the woman who faked her appearance as Madeleine, strives to become the 'true' Madeleine that Scottie so adored:

> The Real is the appearance as appearance, it not only appears WITHIN appearances but it is also NOTHING BUT its own appearance – it is just a certain GRIMACE of reality, a certain imperceptible, unfathomable, ultimately illusory feature that accounts for the absolute difference within the identity.[42]

Madeleine was really there for Scottie, in the faked appearance of Judy as Madeleine; and as a total otherness with regard to Judy she was nothing but this (faked) appearance. The aura that Scottie endows on the faked Madeleine makes her someone other than Judy and this distorted countenance, a grimace, is 'the Real of a pure semblance, of a spectral dimension which shines through our common reality'.[43] What matters is not the objective truth that Madeleine was Judy but the gap that separates the two women and makes them incommensurate: 'There is a truth; everything is not relative – but this truth is the truth of the perspectival distortion as such, not the truth distorted by the partial view from a one-sided perspective.'[44]

With the earlier examples of the human body and Freud's dream about Irma, the Real becomes the raw flesh of mortality, a corporeality at odds with a subjectivity in denial of its own mortality, and at the same time it functions as a disgusting exposure of an elementary life substance called *jouissance* by Lacan (see below). This is not reality's ultimate referent and the Real should not be thought of in this way. The scene in *The Matrix* where Morpheus shows Neo the devastated Chicago landscape ('welcome to the desert of the real') highlights a part of the film's philosophical unsatisfactoriness:

> However, the real is not the 'true reality' behind the virtual simulation, but the void that makes reality incomplete/inconsistent, and the function of every symbolic matrix is to conceal this inconsistency – one of the ways to effect this concealment is precisely to claim that, behind the incomplete/inconsistent reality we know, there is another reality with no deadlock of impossibility structuring it.[45]

One way of approaching the Lacanian real is by way of the working of *objet petit a*. As seen, *objet a* only exists by way of its function in relation to the gap in symbolic reality that it seeks to fill and in this way it is both the gap itself and the object which fills it. This gap goes deeper than the lack that pertains to the subject situated within the symbolic: it is the world itself that lacks consistency, it does not add up, and two analogies provided by Žižek illustrate this. In quantum physics light is modelled as behaving like a particle and like a wave *at the same time*, something that ought to be impossible; in literary fiction, so another example goes, it would be meaningless for the reader of a Sherlock Holmes story to ask how many books are on the shelves in his flat.[46] Reality as we construct it does not make complete sense, there are connecting bits missing from the web of reason and, for the early Žižek, the Real functions as a limit, a negation, countering any construction within the symbolic while also being the gap, the void, around which the symbolic is constructed:

> Lacan's whole point is that the Real is *nothing but* this impossibility of its inscription: the Real is not a transcendent positive entity, persisting somewhere beyond the symbolic order like a hard kernel inaccessible to it ... in itself it is nothing at all, just a void, an emptiness in a symbolic structure marking some central impossibility.[47]

The Real is a consequence of this incompleteness in the ontological landscape and it can be conceived as the unbearable void that *objet petit a* seeks to fill. In this way, *objet petit a* is a deceptive lure: '*a qua* semblance deceives in a Lacanian way: not because it is a deceitful substitute of the Real, but precisely because it invokes the impression of some substantial Real behind it; it deceives by posing as a shadow of the underlying Real'.[48] Part of the illusion sustaining the power of the sublime object, its siren call, comes from imagining it as a surplus part of something that was lost, a prelapsarian part of the Real that was never included in the symbolic order. Integral to an understanding of this illusion is the realization that there is no substantial semblance of the real behind the sublime object: 'However, what we must avoid at any price is conceiving of this left-over as simply secondary, as if we have *first* the substantial fullness of the Real and *then* the process of symbolization.'[49] The Real as a robust fullness that existed before entry into the symbolic world of language is a retroactive construction.

Instead of the Real as some kind of pre-symbolic, proto-reality, the symbolic can be seen to produce from within itself the real.[50]

Instead of being external and anterior the real in this second sense is something posed by and in the symbolic. The very act of referring to the real is a mediation conducted by the symbolic; any account of the real has to take place within language but the real can only be posed and never grasped by language. As a condition within the symbolic it only makes itself felt as a disturbance:[51]

It is not that we need words to designate objects, to symbolize reality, and that then, in surplus, there is some excess of reality, a traumatic core that resists symbolization – this obscurantist theme of the unnameable Core of Higher Reality that eludes the grasp of language is to be thoroughly rejected; not because of a naïve belief that everything can be nominated, grasped by our reason, but because of the fact that the Unnameable is an effect of language.[52]

The register of the Real is associated with the traumatic nature of our entry into language and the abiding feeling that there is something missing in our own subjectivity, something strange and unbanishable at the heart of our identity which cannot be put into words. The Real becomes the ultimate something that the subject renounced when entering the symbolic and it returns as spectral, uncanny apparitions like the slime on the food plate or the view of Irma's throat.[53] As an affect, it can play a part in sustaining a sense of stability by providing 'an answer of the real' to what may otherwise be experienced as a questioning of the stability of our daily life. If the Real can be sensed as safely present in the background, as with the promised experience that fortune telling and horoscopes holds out for the believer, it gives ballast to the unbearable lightness of the subject's experience of self.[54] For the early Žižek, on the other hand, if the proximity of the Real is experienced as being too close then the promised security becomes a nightmare, a traumatic excess that threatens to engulf the symbolic-imaginary realm which provides us with our sense of who we are.

The Real is what accounts for the sublimity that we give to *objet petit a* and this helps explain Žižek's objection to popular forms of Oriental-style spirituality and the 'wisdom' that is claimed to shine forth when objects of desire are recognized as illusory, mere projections of human vanity that we should transcend: 'Even if the object of desire is an illusory lure, *there is a real in this illusion*:

the object of desire in its positive nature is vain, *but not the place it occupies*, the place of the Real, which is why there is more truth in unconditioned fidelity to one's desire than in a resigned insight into the vanity of one's striving.'[55] What this quotation helps to confirm is a pronounced shift in an understanding of the Real, one that rejects seeing it as something unreachable, not to be confronted, and speaks instead of it sometimes having a 'totally fragile appearance: the Real can be something that transpires or shines through ... the problem with the Real is that it happens and *that's* the trauma'.[56]

In a problematic way, arising from the inadequacy of simply bracketing off the Real as something impalpable, a point of impossibility, this talk of it as something that 'happens' brings one back to the difficulty one can have when trying to get to grips with the term and a large part of the difficulty is that the three registers of the imaginary, symbolic and Real are interlinked:

> There are three modalities of the Real: the "real Real" (the horrifying Thing, the primordial object, from Irma's throat to the Alien), the 'symbolic Real' (the real as consistency: the signifier reduced to a senseless formula, like the quantum physics formulas that can no longer be translated back into, or related to, the everyday experience of our life-world), and the 'imaginary real' (the mysterious *je ne sais quoi*, the unfathomable 'something' on account of which the sublime dimension shines through an ordinary object). The Real is thus effectively all three dimensions at the same time: the abyssal vortex that ruins every consistent structure, the mathematized consistent structure of reality, the fragile pure appearance.[57]

Answering why the Real remains so important to Žižek must wait until German idealism is brought into the frame and his ontology and his politics can be seen emerging from a conversation between Hegelian and Lacanian theorizing.

THE THING

In his earlier work, before 1964, Lacan spoke of *das Ding* (the Thing) and Žižek also finds it useful at times to use this term instead of the *little objet a*. The Thing is bound up with the impulse to find something that is felt to have been lost with entry to the symbolic order, an entry that brings about a split between the reality constituted by the symbolic order and the lost Thing. Lacan, when speaking of *das Ding*, makes clear that the object has never been lost, and, for Žižek, because it is a 'mythical object', the paradox is that 'this Thing is retrospectively produced by the very process of symbolization, i.e., that it emerges in the very gesture of its loss'.[58] Desire wants the Thing to be there, to fill the void that burrows its way through subjectivity.

The mother provides the child with a focus, an anchorage for constructing an imaginary consistency, a point of satisfied enjoyment that is cut by the sense of loss when her absence is experienced. In the psychoanalytic world of the infant, the mother becomes its Thing when her attention is periodically withdrawn, when, for example, she attends to her own bodily needs and is not immediately available to satisfy corporeal needs or deeper demands. As Thing, the mother is the inaugural cause of a desire that cannot be met and an object that cannot be attained.

The Thing stands in place of the Lacanian Real, as a threat sometimes of what there might be beyond the limits imposed by symbolization. As a vector, the Thing points back to an intermediary state between animal and human, a void that the subject cannot represent in either the imaginary or the symbolic. This level of being can only be represented in terms of its loss, a deficit which is filled by the *objet a*. Sublimation in classical Freudian theory is a channelling process, a defensive mechanism that directs the libido to find expression in socially acceptable forms such as art but in Lacanian vocabulary sublimation occurs when an ordinary object 'finds itself at the place of the impossible Thing'.[59] In the example of courtly love, the hindrances that prevent direct access to the object being sought, the lady of the knight's quest, are the means whereby an ordinary woman is elevated, sublimated, into a substitute for the Thing.

The Real itself is not an entity but a cause of which the effects appear in a displaced way. The pressure of the Real is sensed in the *objet a* and the Thing comes from the same 'dark domain of the rotary movement of preontological drives'.[60]

DEATH DRIVE

Freud introduced the notion of the death drive as a way of accounting for human behaviour so decidedly at odds with an organism's regard for homeostasis as to be self-destructive. First proposed by him in 1920, in *Beyond the Pleasure Principle*, there is a drive towards death that seeks a return to the inorganic and it persists in the core of human nature. Žižek, following Lacan, does not endorse this view of the death drive as a semi-instinctual force hostile to the libido but, as will be seen in the next chapter, aligns it with Hegelian negativity in a highly original way.

The death drive for Žižek is the insistent yearning for the Real. It is not a wish to die but quite the opposite in the way it constantly seeks something more than mere biological existence. It seeks to reach the Real by filling the gap in the symbolic order, the gap that is itself the Real, but, caught up as it must be in the loop of the signifying chain, this becomes an impossible task, hence the unremitting, never-to-be-satisfied rotation of the death drive. The death drive is emblematic of the fact that humans, unlike animals, are not content with just living. Humans yearn for the Real but are condemned to never finding it and the death drive becomes an excessive attachment to that surplus which cannot be accommodated within the symbolic order of existence. Jenny Diski's description of an ice rink in *Skating to Antarctica* comes close to capturing what Žižek is getting at:

An ice rink is as cruel a reminder of reality as any that has yet been devised. It is a surface artificially constructed to be as friction-free as you can get while having both feet on the ground – yet it is enclosed on all sides by a wooden barrier. An ice rink is a promise made purely for the pleasure of creating disappointment. If you want to skate without stopping you have to go round and round the bounded ice; you can't go on and on, even though the surface permits a gathering of speed which can only be for the purpose of heading forwards without hindrance.[61]

The topology of the death drive is represented by Lacan and by Žižek in ways that can be difficult to grasp, bound up as this drive is with the impenetrability of the Real and the paradox that it is not a desire for death, or at least not death in the earthly sense of finite life coming to an end, but pure desire itself. It is an encounter with the

Real.[62] It incorporates the classical Freudian antagonism between Eros, seen by Žižek as the 'horrifying Real … of the immortal drive', and Thanatos which is viewed as 'the striving to end this horror'.[63] It is an unhinged, insubordinate energy that came into existence in the traumatic interstice between the homeostasis of the creaturely domain and the derailing entry into the language world of *Homo sapiens*.

Žižek locates the space of the death drive by way of the 'dead' subject, embalmed in the chain of signifiers, and that part which escapes the symbolic 'lives' on as something inhuman within the human. This is the 'undead' of horror films, partial objects such as the diabolical red shoes in Anderson's fairy tale that won't stop dancing or the rendering of the voice as a traumatic dimension in *The Exorcist, Testament of Dr Mabuse, The Great Dictator* and *Mulholland Drive*.[64]

This 'undead' libido, called *lamella* by Lacan and conceived as an organ without a body, is described by Žižek as 'the remainder of the life-substance which has escaped the symbolic colonization, the horrible palpitation of the "acephal" drive which persists beyond death, outside the scope of paternal authority, nomadic, with no fixed domicile'.[65] This death drive is immortal and because it is not part of the human world that registers mortality as part of its consciousness it constitutes the 'inhuman' tension that dwells within the human, a 'self-destructive freedom'.[66] The association with freedom is important because the death drive, defying the circumstances that in everyday life contain and curtail our existence, is the source of our autonomy. In this sense it is non-functional, 'an aspect of behaviour that persists beyond any instrumental activity towards achieving certain goals (pleasure, reproduction, wealth, power).'[67] It is for this reason that Žižek can characterize psychoanalysis in non-Darwinian terms, asserting that the death drive is bound up with a failure of human adaptation. Unlike the animal world, there is a level of disconnection between mankind and its natural environment that breaks with determinism, a break in the chain of being, and it is this uncoupling that creates a gap for a pure autonomy.[68]

The excessive and repetitive nature of the death drive results in a strange satisfaction that arises from not reaching our goal. This strange coming together of satisfaction and failure – pleasure in pain – is what Lacan calls *jouissance*.

JOUISSANCE

The French word *jouissance* is commonly translated as enjoyment but using the English word can be misleading in that it suggests satisfied pleasure, whereas for Lacan the term entails an essential excess, a lack of balanced satisfaction, derived from the pleasurable dissatisfaction of never reaching the object of one's desire. *Jouissance* is an experience of the body which can be differentiated from desire in that it is not grounded in loss but thrives on a positive experience, even though this positivity consists in not reaching its goal. Desire and drive can be separated from one another because of the way they relate to *jouissance*:

> Desire stands for the economy in which whatever object we get hold of is 'never *it*', the 'Real Thing', that which the subject is forever trying to attain but which eludes him again and again, while drive stands for the opposite economy, within which the stain of *jouissance* always accompanies our acts.[69]

One psychoanalytic context for *jouissance* is the ideal of the infant to realize a primordial connection of complete oneness with its mother, an ideal that brings loss when the mother's desire becomes problematic but which is never abandoned, forever, holding out the promise of an embodied and full *jouissance*. This myth of absolute *jouissance* operates as a psychic register reckoning actual experiences of enjoyment in a negative key, as something always falling short of the desired ideal. Žižek refers to Lacan's *Seminar XX: Encore*, where the logic of *jouissance* is allied with the logic of the ontological proof of God, to explain the force of this myth. As finite and far from perfect beings, we want to entertain the notion of an absolutely perfect being – God – and because existence must necessarily be part of this perfection it follows that God must indeed exist. Similarly, as beings who always only experience *jouissance* as something partial, never properly realized, we are naturally drawn to the notion of *jouissance* in its entirety: a fullness without any limitation or delay.[70]

Jouissance has an uncanny, spectral quality that haunts the body and mind and Žižek's formulation of this helps explain his fascination with the trope, taken from horror movies, of 'the undead'.

to be 'alive while dead' is to give body to the remainder of Life-Substance which has escaped the symbolic colonization (*lamella*). What we are dealing with here is thus the split between ... the 'dead' symbolic order which mortifies the body and the nonsymbolic Life-Substance of *jouissance*.[71]

Jouissance connects intimately with the Lacanian Real, situating the subject as existentially out-of-place and profoundly alienated. *Jouissance* cannot be divorced from the Real and it shares a precise family resemblance: at a material, physiological level, *jouissance* is that which is structured by the symbolic order; at the same time this process of symbolization produces a leftover, called surplus-enjoyment: 'the trouble with *jouissance* is not that it is unattainable, that it always eludes our grasp, but, rather, that *one can never get rid of it*, that its stain drags along for ever – therein resides the point of Lacan's concept of surplus enjoyment'.[72]

Like the death drive and the whole register of the Real, *jouissance* is bound up with the trauma of human existence. It shares the relentless excess of the death drive, overriding any dynamic stability of the body, disturbing subjectivity by its insistent demands. It possesses ghastly and nauseating qualities that arises from its association with something horribly primordial – indestructible in that it goes beyond any one individual – and viscerally disgusting in a way that is best represented in scenes and sounds from the films of David Lynch or in the voluptuous, hyper-sensuousness of Pre-Raphaelite paintings.[73] In literary fiction, it is given expression in the work of Kafka.[74] At the level of everyday life, we appear as normal beings but social life is a simulacrum behind which 'there lurks an idiot immersed into his solipsistic *jouissance*'.[75]

The subject, says Lacan, is 'in the place from which a voice is heard clamouring "the universe is a defect in the purity of Non-Being" ... This place is called *Jouissance*, and it is the absence of this that makes the universe vain.'[76] The subject is in this empty place and *jouissance*, that which dislocates the apparent stability of those structures which cloak this emptiness, reveals itself in those quirks and aberrations that make the other person unknowable and overwhelmingly different to ourself.[77] It is a fault line that can be traced back to the fundamental rupture in being out of which the subject emerges and this helps account for its disruptive potency and dimension of excess. This potency and excess is employed by fantasy but before looking at the role of fantasy there is another notion, that of the superego, which cannot be divorced from the demands for complete *jouissance*.

SUPEREGO

The term superego was introduced by Freud as an agency within the unconscious that polices the realm of basic, uncoordinated drives that is the id. Lacan's use of superego is counter-intuitive, it is not an agency of censorship although it retains a relationship with law as well as with the severity endowed on it by Freud, a similarity that arises from its roots in anxiety about the enigma of existence, a puzzle that would be answered were we only to attain the mythical promise of a *jouissance* that would thereby solve the riddle of existence. As the Lacanian Bruce Fink cogently expresses it, the persuasive force of this myth insists on making itself felt:

> [I]t *insists* as an ideal, an idea, a possibility thought permits us to envision. In [Lacan's] terminology, it 'ex-sists': it persists outside, as it were. Outside in the sense that it is not a wish [desire], 'Let's do *that* again!' but, rather, 'Isn't there something else you could do, something different you could try?'[78]

Lacan's 'ex-sistence' is the call of the Real, of the Thing that would deliver the impossible fullness of enjoyment, and as such is cannot be openly avowed by the symbolic order.[79] What can be achieved, by way of a compromise that hides the impotence of the big Other but entails a terroristic level of authority over the subject, requires an agency that will ordain a seemingly lawless level of enjoyment but control it by making it an impossible duty: we must enjoy ourselves and at the same time suffer the guilt from failing to attain what is held out as unfailing *jouissance*. This agency is the superego.

The superego can be seen at work in travel book titles such as *Ultimate Experiences for a Lifetime* and *Unforgettable Places to See Before You Die*. The injunction of the superego to enjoy takes various forms and there is something sinister – Žižek likes to label it obscene – about its importuning of what is officially forbidden. And the more we give way to its importuning the greater is the guilt we experience:[80] 'Superego is like the extortioner slowly bleeding us to death – the more he gets, the stronger his hold on us.'[81] The obscenity of the superego resides in the way it allows the symbolic order to solicit what is officially forbidden and what Žižek finds alarming about this is the capacity it possesses to bypass a satisfaction that can come from the *jouissance* of the Other, as illustrated in Adrian Lyne's *Unfaithful* where incipient lesbianism is not a subtext of the film because the two women are heterosexually enjoying the pleasure that comes through sharing a narrative, a sharing that allows *jouissance* to mutually flow between the Other and I.[82] When the superego circumvents this dimension of *jouissance* and imperatively orders enjoyment it takes on, as will be seen, a political force of its own.

FANTASY

Lacan's formula $ \lozenge a$ was introduced (pp. 21-22) apropos the nature of fantasy being the subject's relationship to *objet petit a*. Fantasy arises from the space in the symbolic that remains empty because there is no signifier there that would allow the subject to access itself; hence the permanent lack of self-identity which makes us always out of kilter, askew. Complementing this lack within the subject is the awareness of something missing from the ontological order of reality itself. The fracture in the symbolic construction of reality points to an inconsistency at the level of the ontological – this is the territory of the Real – and fantasy seeks to resolve this inconsistency:

> ... the fundamental fantasy provides the subject with the minimum of being, it serves as a support for his existence – in short, its deceptive gesture is 'Look, I suffer, therefore I am, I exist, I participate in the positive order of being.[83]

Fantasy is the prop that keeps intact our conviction of a meaningful reality and stops us worrying about the number of books on Sherlock Holmes' shelves. The point at which the whole edifice could collapse into meaninglessness is where fantasy operates; another way of saying this is that *objet petit a* locates itself at this point, an empty space which like a bare stage waits for actors, scenery and props, the stuff that each of us in different ways chooses to narrate a sense of who we are. Fantasy is the scene enacted on this stage and it supplies the stage directions indicating what the object of desire is to be: '*though fantasy, we learn how to desire*', as illustrated by Žižek in the science fiction short story 'Store of the Worlds' by Robert

Sheckley.[84] Fantasy tells us what to desire and where we will find that elusive object of our desire or how our *jouissance* has been mislaid, monopolized or misappropriated by others. Filling out the void of $, fantasy is like the bubble wrap and loose paper used to package and protect a fragile item in the post. If the fantasy is directly confronted, traversed, there would be nothing there of substance, for what would remain would be only the *objet petit a*. A subject's fundamental fantasy carries an existential charge and an inbuilt deception of this charge: 'it is precisely this deception of the fundamental fantasy that the act of "traversing the fantasy" serves to dispel: by traversing the fantasy, the subject accepts the void of his nonexistence'.[85] In *The Silence of the Lambs*, according to Žižek, what takes place between Hannibal Lecter (Anthony Hopkins) and Clarice Starling (Jodie Foster) is that he seeks to access Starling's fundamental fantasy – the crying of the lambs and the failure to rescue one of them – in return for helping her capture the serial killer.[86]

Fantasy serves to protect us from an encounter with the Real, and the proximity of the Real finds expression in our dreams: 'it is not that dreams are for those who cannot endure reality, reality itself is for those who cannot endure (the Real that announces itself in) their dreams'.[87] This is how Lacan interprets the dream described by Freud about the father who falls asleep while watching over his son's coffin and wakes up to find that the cloth on the coffin has caught fire. Given the traumatic encounter in the dream with the Real of responsibility for his son's death ('Father, can't you see that I am burning?', asks the son in the dream), the reality of being awake was a means of escape and 'in so far as "dreaming" means fantasizing in order to avoid confronting the Real, the father literally woke up so that he could go on dreaming'.[88] Žižek provides an example of his own in the depiction of war in Spielberg's *Saving Private Ryan* as meaningless slaughter, contrasting it with the notion of fighting a war without causalities to one's own side (like Operation Desert Fox in 1998). Instead of a restrained narrative, a 'symbolic fiction … concealing the Real of senseless bloodbath', bloody and personalized face-to-face violence 'serves as a fantasized protective shield' constructed 'in order to escape the Real of the depersonalized war turned into an anonymous technological apparatus'.[89]

Without the frame of fantasy, claims Žižek, the sexual act would lose what is essential to its allurement and he likes to quote Lacan's statement that there is no such thing as a sexual relationship (*il n'y a pas de rapport sexuel*) in this regard.[90] Sex as something more than copulation requires a level of fantasy and when this breaks down, when the other person is no longer the object-cause of desire, the result is a horrible disintegration of feeling and a collapse into revulsion. One example of Žižek's is Hamlet's changing feelings towards Ophelia in Shakespeare's *Hamlet*; when she ceases to be the object-cause of Hamlet's desire, everything that made her precious to him turns sour: 'life becomes disgusting when our fantasy that mediates our access to it [the Real] disintegrates, so that we are directly confronted with the Real'.[91] The course of events in Hitchcock's *Vertigo* that brings the hero Scottie to realize that the woman Madeleine, the transcendent object of his love, is in fact the less-than-sublime Judy, is read along similar lines.[92] Scottie's realization that he has been duped collapses the fantasy construct that gave density to his being in a way that was not occasioned by his felt shock, earlier in the film, when he thought he had witnessed Madeleine's suicide. In fact, this apparent death crystallized her fantasy role: the melancholy of loss assuaged Scottie's being and gave meaning to his life as he strove to memorialize the image of her grace and beauty. When reality arrives, with the realization that the very ordinary and rather coarse Judy was acting the part of Madeleine all along, faking her apparent suicide as part of her faking of Madeleine, the object as fantasy departs and with the disintegration of *objet a* so too does the hold on his desire that she had become. Something similar accounts for the depressing lack of proper satisfaction in pornography which, by making explicit the sexual act, robs it of what is essential to fantasy: 'Instead of the sublime Thing, we are stuck with vulgar, groaning fornication.'[93]

WHAT AM I?

If the subject relies on fantasy for its selfhood, what substance or depth is there to the self? Over and above the social role play and the whole set of language games assigned and sanctioned by the symbolic order, what is taking place when one subject engages with another that makes us more than mere robots with highly sophisticated programs? When advances in the cognitive sciences and the consequences of the eventual mapping of an individual's genome are also considered, this becomes an even more compelling question.[94] The question here is one version of the 'what is the meaning of life?'

inquiry and while Žižek does not provide any pat answers he does address the value of life:

What makes life 'worth living' is the very *excess of life*: the awareness that there is something for which we are ready to risk our life (we may call this excess 'freedom,' 'honor,' 'dignity,' 'autonomy,' etc.). Only when we are ready to take this risk are we really alive.[95]

This excess, the excess of *jouissance*, far from being pathological is primordial and to disavow it is a denial of life. It is only in moments of the Other's *jouissance*, when one person encounters a little bit of the Real in the other, that intersubjectivity treads on solid ground.[96] In the case of the Neighbour, as will be seen, the trauma of such an encounter becomes a fraught possibility. Putting this to one side for the moment, in any intersubjective experience it is a tiny and apparently inconsequential detail that signals the presence of the Real. Žižek's paradigm for this is the way in which in early American science fiction films the presence of aliens in the otherwise normal life of a small town can only be detected by some minor detail. The small difference between the alien and non-alien would seem hardly to matter and yet it is of crucial importance. Hitchcock's *Vertigo* is alluded to again in this context because of the way both Madeleine, the woman worshipped by Scottie but really someone else in disguise, and Judy, the woman persuaded by Scottie to impersonate Madeleine and who it turns out was all along the 'real' Madeleine, are both fakes and yet the difference between the two of them 'renders all the more palpable the absolute otherness of Madeleine with regard to Judy ...'.[97] This otherness is the appearance of the Real but it is nothing more than appearance and lacks any substantial property: it is 'a certain imperceptible, unfathomable, ultimately illusory feature that accounts for the absolute difference within the identity'.[98] When, at the end of the film, Scottie fully realizes that Judy and Madeleine were identical, he is finally able to face the abyss that was haunting his being (his fear of heights being the symptom of this), the empty centre of the symbolic order that is filled by the fantasy object: 'We have this same experience every time we look into the eyes of another person and feel the depth of his gaze.'[99]

The otherness is the illusory object of desire but as the earlier quotation about truth residing in fidelity to one's desire sought to make clear (pp. 28–29) there is a precious and authentic quality to this sense of the Real inhabiting another person; it is akin to what Benjamin called an *aura*[100] and it is what comes into play, for example, when making the distinction between a great actor and a mediocre one.[101] Žižek's own and more alarming example comes from imagining a situation where parents opt for the cloning of a child they have lost. This second child would be experienced as an abominable ersatz despite, or because of, its identical appearance to the first child. What would be missing would be that inexplicable *je ne sais quoi*, Lacan's *objet petit a*, that makes one person different from another.[102] Notwithstanding the libidinal force behind it, this *objet petit a*, it must be emphasized, is only 'the real me' in so far as it represents the subject's need to find some niche in the big Other. Given its own lack and inconsistency, however, the big Other cannot offer a properly substantial haven and it is this void that the subject is identifying with through the *objet*.[103]

Jouissance is part of the frame of understanding around questions of intersubjectivity and the Other but, as will be seen, *jouissance* can also be brought to the fore when explaining what lies behind a particular instance of the ideological. In another context, the same term is pinpointed as the ahistorical, disturbing nugget of enjoyment that defines what it means to be human.[104] What lies behind the compound ways Žižek employs a concept like *jouissance* is the fact that the three registers of human experience – the imaginary, symbolic and real – do not lend themselves to neat compartmentalization. Lacan used the mathematician's Borromean rings (remove one and the other two become unlinked) as an analogy for the way they are necessarily chained together. This mapping of one of these realms onto another was instanced earlier in relation to configurations of the Lacanian Real. Žižek's account of the neighbour is another example of this interrelationship.

WHAT IS MY NEIGHBOUR?

In the imaginary sphere, the neighbour is comfortingly recognizable as a being like myself. At the symbolic level the neighbour and I operate within the same social rules and conduct ourselves before the big Other in a basically similar manner. Yet there is an inhuman quality that resides in all humans, a core of being that pertains to the Real, prior to the Name of the Father and the anguished separation from the maternal body. This Thing is meaningless, inaccessible yet frighteningly close. This Real is the Neighbour, capitalized sometimes by Žižek to emphasize a presence in this uncanny mode that constitutes for me a source of anxiety. The Neighbour is a subject of his own experiences, not mine, and the distance this creates between us can be felt as nauseating; my neighbour's way of materializing his *jouissance* is unlike mine and, when this awareness makes itself felt too closely, the hold I have on my own way of life is disturbed.

In different ways, the imaginary and the symbolic keep at bay the traumatic presence of the neighbour *qua* the Real. The imaginary other, as opposed to the Other, mirrors my quotidian sense of self and invites reciprocity and mutual engagement but this smoothing of differences can only take place within the symbolic and impersonal realm of shared meanings and customs. If the symbolic is missing, the agreeable neighbour appears as the monstrous Thing. But a presence of the Real is also required to be there because without some part of it answering to our needs we would be lifeless, mere ciphers conducting exchanges at the symbolic level. The three registers, then, interrelate and interlock.[105]

The monstrosity of the Neighbour is what differentiates Žižek's account of the face from that associated with the philosopher Levinas, a difference Žižek highlights to signal the incommensurability of their views.[106] Both see the Other as wholly inaccessible but for Levinas the encounter with the face of the Other brings forth an awareness of vulnerability and a non-reciprocal call of responsibility for their plight. This non-voluntary call, an ethical epiphany, accesses the absolute alterity of the Other, it is an infinite responsibility defining subjectivity and preceding any ontological category. The Other's face takes me hostage by the force of its unknowability and renders the ethical dimension.

Levinas' concept of the face is, for Žižek, a fetish that, by offering a non-linguistic window into the soul of the Other, disguises the abyssal circulation of signifiers that makes up the symbolic order.[107] For Žižek, the face does not reveal the transcendent but helps us hide from the monstrosity that is the Neighbour; it is a mask that gentrifies the horror of the neighbour as Thing and, instead of confronting the abyss of the Other, the face allows us to compose the neighbour as a fellow human with whom we can empathize:

We say the eye is the window of the soul but what if there is no soul behind the eye, what if the eye is a crack through which we can perceive just the abyss of a netherworld?[108]

The face cannot serve as a mask when it is completely hidden, anxiety arises when seeing someone wearing a full-body veil, and Žižek argues that it is the burqa as an embodiment of the horror of the Other that underlies the disquiet behind calls for banning it – not 'official' reasons to do with women's dignity.[109]

The anxiety that can accompany a too-close proximity to the neighbour is, of course, the same anxiety that the neighbour may feel towards ourself. The unknowable Thing that is in the Neighbour is ourself and to say that 'the Other *qua* another person is ontologically unknowable' is to say that we cannot know ourselves.[110] A related aspect of this is the shock that can accompany the experience of being the beloved, sensing the gap between I as experienced by myself and I as someone with 'the unfathomable X in me which causes love'.[111]

The proverb about good fences making for good neighbours captures Žižek's point that there is an optimum distance to be maintained between ourselves and others. One reason he highlights Chaplin's *City Lights* is that its ending poses the unsettling nature of the neighbour by having the girl recognize the tramp as her benefactor, leaving the audience to wonder how she will deal with the person who no longer inhabits the symbolic role she had mistakenly attributed to him.[112] The big Other provides a mode for misidentifying with others, disallowing the Other to get too close, and *City Lights* ends with the girl facing the tramp without this safety net.

To encounter one's neighbour too closely can be experienced as a form of harassment and for Žižek there is a contemporary obsession with constructing fences and keeping a proper distance between oneself and one's neighbour.[113] One underlying cause of this obsession arises from clothing the ambivalence of the neighbour in an ideological dress and employing it politically as a fear of the Other. The obverse of this fear, as will be seen later, is a recognition of the inhuman core of human existence and making this part of the basis for an ethics and an emancipatory politics.

IDEOLOGY

Žižek's application of Lacanian terms to social and cultural life is especially convincing in his accounts of how ideology works in a 'post-ideological' age where the horizon of understanding is so completely dominated by capitalism that entire fields of what would once have been considered seditious have been incorporated into everyday culture: 'the emperor is naked and the media trumpet forth this fact, yet nobody seems really to mind – that is, people continue to act as if the emperor were not naked'.[114] In the past, proclaiming the nakedness of the emperor was an illicit act and any enjoyment that might attach itself to such an awareness was subject to the guilt-inducing agency of the Freudian superego. Transgression and its enjoyment is now a command of the superego and it masks an underlying allegiance to authority, making it difficult to discern and to practise authentic dissent.

This pre-emption of dissent is the world of Mark Fisher's capitalist realism, where token anti-capitalism is just more grist to the Hollywood mill and 'alternative' signifies just another style;[115] a world where transgression is so marketable that couples who stay together for life are the 'true subversives' and a film like *Forrest Gump*, that could be viewed for a subversive effect, openly reveals the secret of ideology.[116] What were once potential areas of resistance and contention have been neutralized, absorbed into a milieu and only extremes are allowed to be designated as ideological.[117] All the while though, Žižek argues, ideology operates at the level of the unconscious and engages the subject's libido; it is not an illusion masking the truth 'but that of an (unconscious) fantasy structuring our social reality itself'.[118] What allows people to think they're 'so clever and classless and free'[119] is not to be found in their articulation of conscious beliefs, a basic point that Žižek likes to make by recounting the joke about the patient who thought he was a grain of seed and might be eaten by a hungry chicken. He was cured by psychiatrists and released from hospital but immediately returned, trembling with fear. The doctor is puzzled and asks if he does not now know he is not a grain of seed: ' "Of course I know," replies the patient, "but does the chicken?" '[120] Put another way, 'we "feel free" because we lack the very language to articulate our unfreedom.'[121]

Even when cynicism about capitalism passes for common sense, people behave as if they believe in the illusions they so confidently dismiss. Indeed, it is *because* we can adopt an ironic distance towards certain beliefs that we can actually behave as if in thrall to them. An individual's cynical attitude of disbelief is a genuine subjective experience but the same person's outward behaviour is thoroughly compliant because it springs from a disavowed attachment to the prevailing law. People believe in something because they are able to think they don't believe in it; conscious disowning fastens unconscious belief, as with the Calvinist notion of Predestination and the belief that everything is already decided. This makes us passive victims of Fate, it would seem, yet it facilitated the frenetic activity that bootstrapped capitalism: 'We act all the time in order to sustain the big Other's (in this case God's) fixity.'[122]

Žižek's personal experience of this kind of paradox came from living under Really Existing Socialism, the de facto socialism of Yugoslavia, where most people were well aware of the inadequacies and subterfuges of the system but carried on as if they believed the ideology and lacked knowledge of how matters really stood. Žižek likes to explain this in terms of what the big Other knows or does not know. In Yugoslavia, it was the big Other that did not know what most people privately knew. It is only when the illusion of the big Other's ignorance is broken, as when, for example, Khrushchev made his speech in 1956 denouncing Stalin's crimes, that the forces maintaining the status quo lose their efficacy. Most of the Soviet nomenclature were cynical manipulators with few illusions about the Stalinist regime they served but they had displaced belief onto the Big Other 'which, as it were, believed on their behalf. Now their proxy had disintegrated.'[123] In a 'non-ideological' age like our own, belief also functions at a distance: it is the thinking that we are removed from an ideological identity that enables the ideology to exert a hold on us, as with the crew in *MASH* who are maintaining the military machine not despite but because of their healthy cynicism and ironic play, or the soldier in *Full Metal Jacket* who seems not to identify with military life but ends up shooting a wounded Vietcong girl.[124]

The unconscious, through which ideology works, is not to be thought of as residing in some deep basement of subjectivity but rather as there at ground level, outside on the pavement not behind some pathologically closed door of the personal self. The unconscious is embodied in our behaviour and materialized in social institutions; psychoanalysis is not psychology and so, for example, 'Eichmann himself didn't really have to hate the Jews; he was able to be just an ordinary person. It's the objective ideological machinery that did the hating; the hatred was imported, it was "out there".'[125] In a similar spirit, Žižek identifies an essential falsity in Spielberg's *Schindler's List* because of the way it reduces the horrors of Nazism to the individual psychology of the camp commander.[126]

What are the libidinal factors at work in ideology? As seen, lack and a sense of loss are inherent to desire and they accompany desire's restless move from one object to another. The fact that there is nothing positive that can ever replace its constitutive lack means that desire can only be set in motion by an object, the *objet petit a*, that embodies this deficiency and which is invested with a sublimity it does not possess. It can be called sublime because the promise it holds out for the subject is the attainment of a meaningful and whole place and it this pledge of ultimate consistency that makes the *objet petit a* the great desideratum, 'the sublime object of ideology'. The recognition of such an object is not obvious – there are no special glasses, as in John Carpenter's film *They Live* that enable us to directly see ideology[127] – and it needs looking at askew in order to see its ideological contours.

At a fundamental ideological level, it is society's class struggle – the antagonism between a desire for solidarity and the capitalist drive to compete and divide – that marks the impossibility, the lack, that needs to be filled in and given body by a seemingly positive object. Such an object is the sublime object of ideology and Žižek's definitive example in this regard is the figure of the Jew in anti-Semitism. The social field is ridden by an inconsistency – a wished-for state of organic, conflict-free integration colliding with the fact of class divisions – and the figure of the Jew embodies this impossibility by an inversion of what is actually the case: instead of acknowledging the fundamental antagonism as the source of society's failure to achieve harmony, the Jew is blamed for the social ill and functions as a fetish giving body to the inconsistency.[128]

A Lacanian refinement is given to the way ideology operates by way of anamorphosis, a deformation that only takes on a familiar appearance when viewed from a particular point. Lacan's example is Holbein's *The Ambassadors* where the skull can only be seen when viewed awry; such a gaze is the point where the subject's distortion, created by the desire for a plenitude represented in the painting by the ambassador's riches, is seen to be inscribed into the picture: 'showing us', says Lacan, 'that, as subjects, we are literally called into the picture, and represented here as caught'.[129] The objective reality, that of human finitude, is brought together with the subjective twist that sees only material wealth; in this way the subjective warp is reflected back into the subject matter of the picture and rendered 'objective'. Similarly, the anti-Semite, experiencing life as disorganized and confused, looks at the figure of the Jew and sees an explanation that makes it all clear.

It is not so much that the anti-Semitic sees the Jew as mercenary, dirty, sinister and so on, but that the Jews are seen like this '*because they are Jews*' – they possess some ineffable quality that makes them so – and a way of understanding this deep-rooted racism is to recognize the libidinal force of *objet petit a* at work.[130] The psychoanalytic roots of anti-Semitism, and racism more generally, are bound up with the nature of *jouissance* and the unfulfilled pleasure that is an essential part of it. The feeling that there is something just beyond our reach accounts for an abiding discontent on the part of the subject and it feeds into the mind's notion that someone else, the Other, might possess a level of *jouissance* denied to ourselves. A community is held together by a 'shared relationship toward a Thing, toward Enjoyment incarnated', nationalism is an eruption of just such enjoyment, while the racist nationalist is unconsciously in thrall to the idea that others have stolen our *jouissance*.[131] Domiciled in the unconscious is the idea that the foreigner has either taken or is planning to take *objet petit a* from us or possesses a closer relationship to it than we do. Racist violence is a way of dealing with the threat;[132] postmodern racism, discreetly cloaked in liberal ideology by a virtuous multiculturalism, is more nuanced by tolerating the 'folklorist Other' – ethnic cuisines, local customs and peculiarities, and the like – by the 'regulation of its *jouissance*; that is, the "real Other" is by definition "patriarchal", "violent", never the Other of ethereal wisdom and charming custom'.[133] This celebration of the innocuous is a sieve that strains off anything that might truly disturb, as in Michael Palin's television travelogues, and 'amounts to postmodern racism at its most essential'.[134]

Jouissance can also be a factor in the support of an ideology, not openly but by permitting subjects to experience desires they would prefer not to be made public. This is allowed for by the law's Janus-like ability to present two faces: the official mandate to regulate social peace is its public visage but at the same time it looks in the opposite direction and unofficially suspends this mandate and endorses transgression. This is Žižek's understanding of how the superego –fictionally in the film *A Few Good Men*, historically real in the Ku Klux Klan – maintains the ideology of a group (the racism of white communities in the American South, the *esprit de corps* of the military) by allowing unofficially for transgressive acts to occur.[135] The law calls for subjects to forego *jouissance* in the higher interest of the public good and an ideology is at its most effective when it conceals a shadowy underside (Žižek labels it the 'obscene supplement') that allows subjects to suspend the official law and participate in a guilty enjoyment under the pretence of a social normality.[136] It is in this sense that the tortures at Abu Ghraib, which were neither directly ordered nor individual aberrations, functioned as an initiation '*into American culture*, they [Iraqi prisoners] got the taste of its obscene underside which forms the necessary supplement to the public values of personal dignity, democracy, and freedom'.[137]

CHAPTER THREE

ŽIŽEK AND GERMAN IDEALISM

The idea that our experience of the world is mediated by categories of thought, that we are not passive observers of a world that is simply there and given to us, no longer strikes us as novel. It originates with Kant (1724–1804), and Hegel (1770–1831) accepted it but was only prepared to follow it a certain distance and he gave it his own radical inflection. German idealism, as a term that includes Hegel, but also Fichte (1762–1814), Schelling (1775–1854) and a number of other thinkers, preconditions subjectivity as the basis for the 'objectivity' of the world but seeks to negotiate the often troubling ramifications of this relationship in the light of Kant's philosophy. For Hegel, human beings produce their identity, their world and thought is self-grounding; as he put the matter in his *Lectures on the Philosophy of World History*:

> the spirit is essentially active; it makes itself into that which it is in itself, into its own deed, its own creation. In this way, it becomes its own object, and has its own existence before it.[1]

At a very general philosophical level, idealism is the view that thought determines the nature of the world. Taken to an extreme, as it was by Bishop Berkeley, this could entail a denial of any physical reality outside of our minds. It is also the case, however, that idealism can accept a material world while stressing the defining role of thought and reason, downplaying the physical world's independence from mental ideas. German idealism is of this kind and is espoused by Žižek with an ontological emphasis of his own: 'The point is not that there is no reality outside our mind, the point is rather that there is no mind outside reality.'[2] It is because we are part of reality that we can never be in a neutral position to observe it objectively; like the embedded journalists in the Iraq war, our position is part of what is observed and if this distorting perspective is removed then so too is the object of the observation. This is quite different from fashionable postmodernist thought which celebrates the plurality of different subject positions and the play of *différance* while taking for granted the existence of an underlying, homogenous world. Žižek's ontology entails a universe that is necessarily fissured and inconsistent, not fully realized, although not because our knowledge is mind-based, which it is, but because this is the way the world is.

To arrive at an understanding of this position involves starting out, as Žižek sometimes does when explaining his take on the world, from Kant's revolution in philosophy. Kant's transcendental turn, universally recognized as an epochal event in philosophy, was a moment of revelation for Žižek when he first experienced its intellectual force: 'the world is not simply the universe or everything that exists … understanding what the world is means, in transcendental terms, understanding some pre-existing, at least historically, a priori structure which determines how we understand how the world is disclosed to us. This for me is the crucial turn.'[3]

THE TRANSCENDENTAL TURN

Kant set himself the challenge of outlining the scope of human reason in order to establish whether metaphysics could count as knowledge, as opposed to being merely an attitude or belief. The initial task, defining what counts as knowledge, is addressed in the first sentence of the introduction to *Critique of Pure Reason* when he asserts that there 'can be no doubt that all our knowledge begins with experience'.[4] Experience is possible because of our senses; what we see, hear, touch, smell and taste, says Kant, is where our knowledge *begins*. The senses provide us with intuitions and what is present to us in this way – what we intuit – is what Kant calls 'appearances'. Like any beginning, this is only the first part of something and one expects there to be more to knowledge than just appearances. This something else is also defined in his introduction to *Critique of Pure Reason*: 'I entitle transcendental all knowledge which is occupied not so much with objects as with the mode of our knowledge of objects in so far as this mode of knowledge is to be possible *a priori*.'[5] Transcendental can be taken to mean that which comes before experience and it is Kant's transcendental turn, the insight that our view of the world is necessarily mediated and that reality in itself cannot ever be directly accessed, that is of momentous importance to Žižek.

Kant is praised by Žižek for detecting the 'crack in the ontological edifice of reality',[6] an assessment that is drawn from some of the essentials of Kant's philosophy; in particular, the division he makes between two distinct orders of reality – the phenomenal and the noumenal – and the consequent difference between things in themselves and things as they appear to us. Our senses provide us with something about the world outside of ourselves but it does not follow that what we intuit is a pure and unqualified awareness of whatever it is that causes our senses to experience something in the first place.

The mind makes an order of the phenomenal, the knowable physical world of appearances, by transforming what it intuits with concepts of the understanding, forms of thought that Kant calls 'categories'. Such categories, examples of which are the concepts of substance and that of cause, possess a truth that is presupposed. Without these forms of thought, Kant states, the world would not be intelligible to us: 'they relate of necessity and *a priori* to the objects of experience, for the reason that only by means of them can any object whatsoever of experience be thought'.[7] It follows for Kant that any object encountered through our senses must have a cause, even if in a particular case the cause may not be known to us, because this is an a priori condition, a 'transcendental' condition of the experience of objects. These categories of thought are not generated through a process of abstraction based on our experiences but spontaneously by our understanding. They do not 'mirror' the true nature of objects but they insist on what can be counted as an object by us.

Kant carefully sets out the different cognitive levels involved in transforming what is intuited into what is understood and imagination is identified as one of the mediating faculties involved. The imagination is placed between a pure manifold of sensuous intuition and the unifying ability of the understanding:

> What must first be given – with a view to the *a priori* knowledge of all objects – is the *manifold* of pure intuition; the second factor involved is the *synthesis* of this manifold by means of

the imagination. But even this does not yield knowledge. The concepts which give *unity* to this pure synthesis, and which consist solely in the representation of this necessary synthetic unity, furnish the third requisite for the knowledge of an object; and they rest on the understanding.[8]

Objects, then, can only be known to us through the way they appear in accordance with the forms of thought; they cannot be known in themselves. Given, though, that we are able to think of the idea of things in themselves, though not through our senses, it is reasonable to give a name for such a concept. Kant's term for this is noumena, the plural of noumenon. The noumenal refers to things-in-themselves, about which we can think but never actually know; and because they cannot be known, as Kant states, the 'concept of a noumenon is a merely *limiting concept*, the function of which is to curb the pretensions of sensibility; and it is therefore only of negative employment'.[9]

Kant is very aware of the danger, having introduced noumena as opposed to phenomena, of seeming to present a two-fold picture of what lies outside of ourselves. It is easy to fall into mistakenly supposing that what we see, phenomena, is in some way a pale imitation of what really lies hidden from our view, the noumenal world. Kant is not saying this, or even suggesting it as a possibility. The world we experience is not some kind of illusion, or some inferior version of what is really 'real'. His point is that what we experience is necessarily based on what appears *to us* and appearances, as appearances, can only be in us and not in the things themselves. Kant's 'thing-in-itself' allows for the awareness of a subjective space between what is experienced and the one doing the experiencing while at the same time providing an objective and strenuous basis to the givenness of reality.

For Žižek, philosophy proper begins with Kant's transcendental turn, the bringing to light of the horizon of intelligibility within which being exists, and in particular with Kant's recognition (an anticipation of Lacan's $) of the subject as irresolvedly divided.[10] Kant undermines the idea that the 'I think' of Descartes' *cogito ergo sum* (I think therefore I am) reveals a self-transparent identity that can constitute the subject as a substantial self:

Through this I or he or it (the thing) which thinks, nothing further is represented than a transcendental subject of the thoughts = X. It is known only through the thoughts which are its predicates, and of it, apart from them, we cannot have any concept whatsoever ...[11]

Kant is here remarking on the nature of the 'I ... which thinks', the concept he calls 'transcendental apperception', a unified consciousness that precedes the reception of intuitions from the phenomenal world, and which is required by the 'categories' in order to regulate past, present and future intuitions. Kant distinguishes this unknowable 'I', the Kantian subject, from the merely empirical self of phenomenal life. The Kantian subject cannot access its own ontological essence, its self-reflexiveness is strictly limited in this respect, but although we cannot experience this unified self it must be there to unify the temporal and sensation-based flux and thus avoid 'merely a blind play of representations, less even than a dream'.[12] The transcendental unity of apperception is the necessary condition of knowledge that underlies the work of the categories that rule our representations.

Žižek seizes on the difficulties caused for Kant by trying to see the subject as both noumenal and phenomenal. The noumenal-like subject that makes experience possible cannot appear as a phenomenon, an appearance, to itself but neither, as the lines above from the *Critique of Pure Reason* make clear, can it appear to itself as itself.[13] The paradox is that this 'I' of apperception, the subject, can only be identified in terms of the impossibility of knowing what it is; reminding Žižek of that moment in *Blade Runner* when Deckard, discovering that Rachael is a replicant but doesn't herself realize it, asks 'How can it not know what it is?'[14]

In order to follow Žižek's account of Kant and Hegel, some acquaintance with Kant's antinomies is necessary. Antinomies arise for Kant due to the ability of reason to derive a proposition and its negation in ways that seem equally convincing. The first antinomy arises from asserting that the world must have a temporal beginning and a spatial limit, reason would suggest this must be the case, while intuition (time and space for Kant are necessary and pure forms of intuition, the grounds of possibility for everything we experience, making it impossible to posit a position existing outside, beyond, time and space) points to a world with no beginning in time or limit in space. Another antinomy arises from asserting that the parts making up a composite substance must be finite yet also maintains that the parts are infinite in number. The third antinomy is the conflict between there being a cause for everything that takes place and a freedom that is purely spontaneous. The final antinomy arises from asserting that the infinite chain of causes excludes any being that necessarily accounts for this while at the same time thinking there has to be a first cause: a being that provides the ground for everything that is contingent. For Kant, these antinomies are the result of the futile attempt to go beyond experience, to think there is a vantage point from where the totality can be seen. For Hegel, as will be seen, some of these antinomies point to a basic ontological inconsistency.

LACAN IN KANT

The Kantian subject lacks not only knowledge of itself but of the whole noumenal world that lies beyond the scope of the phenomenal. Reality is constituted by the transcendental subject but a true understanding of it remains an a priori limitation of human existence. Kant's giant step forward in philosophy can be seen not only in the acceptance of an inherent epistemological limitation but also the acknowledgement that it brings in its wake of a corresponding ontological insufficiency. There is a lack of substantiality to the subject *and* a space in constituted, phenomenal reality created by the inaccessibility of the noumenal. It is the split that Kant creates between the phenomenal world of experience and a noumenal beyond that is important and Žižek illustrates this importance with a Magritte painting, *La lunette d'approche*, of a half-open window showing in the window's closed part a blue sky with clouds but in the open part, through which we directly see external reality without the glass intervening, nothing but a characterless black mass. The painting is a 'staging of the "Kantian" split between (symbolized, categorized, transcendentally constituted) reality and the void of the Thing-in-itself, of the Real, which gapes open in the midst of reality and confers upon it a fantasmatic character'.[15]

The kinship that is drawn by Žižek between Kant and Lacan is not readily allowed for in orthodox readings of Kant. The conventional view of Kant stresses his separation of epistemology from ontology, his demarcation of their respective territories so as to show the illegitimacy of making metaphysical claims based on our necessarily limited knowledge of the world. Contrarily, Žižek insists on the connection which he sees made manifest in Kant's transcendental idealism between an ontological gap in reality and the ontological void that defines the subject itself: the noumenal and the phenomenal distinction is placed *within* the phenomenal.[16] This goes to the heart of Žižek 's ontology, the full import of which will become clearer when Schelling and Hegel are brought into the frame and placed alongside his Lacanian understanding of the antagonism, the lack of integration, inherent to the whole of reality, including human nature.

There is a parallel for Žižek between, on the one hand, the contradictions and deadlocks within the Kantian subject and, on the other, the split in the Lacanian subject between a symbolic identity and the noumenal-like force of desire constituted by lack. Similarly, there is a parallel between the ontological insufficiency of reality itself – the number of books on Sherlock Holmes' shelf cannot be known (p. 27) – and Kant's transcendentally constituted world. The philosophical breakthrough achieved by Kant is seen to be the positioning of subjectivity inside a reality that is characterized by a kind of stalemate due to human finitude.

For Lacan, the gap that gives rise to the noumenal only arises because of the way the signifier intervenes within the field of desire. The signifying system structures our reality symbolically and in doing so creates the gap that separates us from 'the void of the Real, the index of the lost Thing'.[17] We seek the Thing, the object of desire which would harmonize the drive. The Kantian epistemological lack (of the 'thing-in-itself') relates to and depends on the peculiarity of desire's logic: because of the inadequacy of the signifying process, desire produces retroactively the Thing. The conclusion is that there is nothing behind the phenomenal screen, only the subject shaping the Thing and illegitimately giving it a substance once we deceive ourselves into thinking it existed before our sense of loss.

Žižek's argument is that Kant failed to follow through on the implications of his own radical insights, the possibility that if the curtain of phenomena were drawn aside instead of the substantial thing-in-itself being presented, there would only be the phantasmagorical forms placed there by our gaze. But German idealism, principally in the work of Schelling and Hegel, did not make this mistake. These two philosophers develop an idealism that does not require the noumenal Thing-in-itself existing beyond our rationality but Žižek wishes to stress how the philosophical genesis of what they come to say lies nascently with Kant and the split that results from a reality that never reveals its totality.

SCHELLING

It was the German idealist philosopher Fichte who took the brave step of rejecting the idea of objects 'in themselves', unable to be experienced directly, and sought a groundless theory of knowledge that favours the self-determining subject and what he calls 'intellectual intuition': 'it is that whereby I know something because I act'.[18] The subject posits itself in its own mind but exists in relation to other subjects. Schelling, who much admired the work of Fichte although later disagreement arose between them, develops the self-positing of the subject but locates its expression in the living force of nature and raises metaphysical questions about subjectivity and its emergence from a material basis that from a strictly Kantian point of view are inadmissible: 'How it happens that things come to be represented at all, about that there is the deepest silence.'[19]

Like Fichte, Schelling is also not content with Kant's thing-in-itself as an inaccessible unknown and seeks to probe ways of being by distinguishing between an eternally past 'Ground' (that which precedes transcendentally constituted reality) and present 'Existence' (experiential reality). Kant, recognizing the category mistake that would be entailed by trying to apply our constituted knowledge to that which precedes experience, cordons off epistemology from ontology. Schelling, though, is not satisfied with this demarcation. He wants to know how, so to speak, beginning began; and providing an answer means accounting for the origin of time. This is accomplished by equating the start of linear time with a foundational and decisional moment – In the Beginning was the Word – which initiates the temporal flow of change. With the Beginning, the moment of decision is a demarcating of the present from the past, the passage to the Symbolic.

The question is in what way does this moment of creation arise from the abyss of Ground.[20] How is a distance created within the In-itself, a splitting that allows it to appear to itself? How, in other words, did we pass from immersion in nature to subjectivity? There is a 'vanishing mediator', a withdrawal from reality that creates the space for a symbolic order. God provides Schelling with a way of addressing this vortex of nothingness, a God that contemplates its own nonbeing and wills nothing, yet is caught in and driven by an immanent contradiction. The nature of this contradiction is to be found in the way that the tranquillity of willing nothingness is at the same time, as an act of will, something positive and actualizing. The act of willing can be envisaged as a position at the top of a seesaw, a moment of expansion but one that is always accompanied by a contractive urge, the bottom of the seesaw, to annihilate anything that could possibly become something. Žižek has two comparisons for this unbalanced state, where un-integrated being yearns to escape its self-enclosed and self-repeating oscillation. The first one is that of a trapped animal tightening its snare every time it tries to leap out of it, yet condemned to repeat an attempted escape; the second is the cosmological principle of a tenuous balance between the expansion of the universe and the contraction of gravitational force.[21]

This antagonism of forces within Ground is outside of time, a form of Nothing that precedes reason and the causal network, and it is only by way of their discharge into an eternal past that linear time – history – is inaugurated. What takes place is a self-positing act, outside of time and preceding consciousness, whereby we choose our eternal character; an act of contracting one's being. In theological terms, man predestines himself. Such a beginning, like Baron Münchhausen pulling himself out of the swamp just by lifting himself by the hair, is a paradox: the self-positing is already done, it is in the past, but a past that was never present.

It is the Word, language, that intercedes in and mediates the antagonism between expansion and contraction and Žižek glosses Schelling's account in terms of the Word's expansive ability to contract the speaker's being outside of itself: 'In the (verbal) sign I *find myself outside of myself*, as it were; I posit my unity outside myself, in a signifier that represents me.'[22]

Žižek finds in Schelling's philosophy a prescient and materialist account of subjectivity's genesis as an emergence from the Real of unformed, incomplete matter, 'primordial, pre-symbolic, inchoate "stuff"' (what in *Finnegans Wake* Joyce calls "chaosmos").[23] He interprets Ground as the rotary motion of drives – metaphorizing its primordial dysfunctioning as the agitated driving of the bus in the film *Speed*[24] – and where Schelling's account has a theosophical narrative, in which God is initially incomplete and only by negating a part of himself, self-creating a distance from the drives, does he become fully himself and thereby institute true beginning, Žižek's construction has a psychoanalytic plotline: 'the true Beginning is the passage from the "closed" rotary motion to "open" progress, from drive to desire – or, in Lacanian terms, from the Real to the Symbolic'.[25] What is an 'undifferentiated pulsation of drives'[26] is contracted into the symbolic order and what is left behind, the 'remainder' referred to in the title of Žižek's book on Schelling (*The Indivisible Remainder*), is the circling around the *objet a* by the drive, the fantasy of restoring an immediacy that has been lost. The symbolic order as a whole mirrors the way the identity of the arbitrary signifier stands for its opposite, pure difference, and this means that the subject alienates himself in language; something is gained (by leaving behind the abyss of nothingness) and something is lost (by taking on the contingency of that which is not the same as itself) in the transition from Ground to Existence. Schelling is thus seen to anticipate Lacan's formulation of the barred subject, $.[27]

An important part of the richness of Schelling's thought, for Žižek, resides in its account of human freedom emerging out of the traumatic transition from Ground to Existence. The genesis of freedom becomes an abyssal, frightening act in Schelling and it gives Žižek scope to add another layer of meaning to the Real. The Real, as outlined earlier in Chapter Two, can be experienced as something revolting, palpitating raw flesh, the extraterrestrial from *Alien*[28] but what if this sense of the ghastly lurking Thing is itself a veil, hiding something even more unbearable? The heart of darkness for Žižek is a Conradian horror and it emanates from the unconditioned, abyssal freedom of the pre-ontological, a-temporal Real, out of which emerges the subject:

> ... this primordial Freedom which, by means of its contraction, gets entrapped into the vicious cycle of its own self-imposed chains, in man blows these chains asunder and regains itself. In other words: human freedom is actual, not just an illusion due to our ignorance of the necessity that effectively governs our lives ...[29]

Determinism ('the necessity that effectively governs our lives') is not seen to provide a satisfactory account for the development of autonomous subjectivity. This is why, in another context, addressing issues in the cognitive sciences, Žižek speaks of consciousness emerging as a response to the ontological realm of primordial freedom. Consciousness is not bound up with the evolution of the species but comes about as a kind of malfunction resulting unintentionally from an encounter with the Real of total, meaningless freedom:

> Original awareness is impelled by a certain experience of failure and mortality – a kind of snag in the biological weave. And all the metaphysical dimensions concerning humanity, philosophical self-reflection, progress and so on emerge ultimately because of this basic traumatic fissure.[30]

It is in Hegel that Žižek finds the most compelling account of this 'traumatic fissure'.

HEGEL

Žižek takes pains to distance himself from the view of Hegel as a thinker who develops a global, totalizing system expressing the world's rational and homogenous structure. The Hegelian dialectic, he repeatedly stresses, is not a teleological process that encompasses difference in a self-mediating movement onwards and upwards towards the absolute Idea, a final synthesis called 'absolute knowledge'. For Žižek, Hegel's Absolute is not some conclusive meeting of knowledge with Truth because there is no substantial In-Itself called Truth and the dialectical process does not lead to a final totality. An aspect of Žižek's heterodox reading of Hegel may be briefly illustrated at this stage by a consideration of how necessity, the sense that something had to happen because it was fated to do so, can only arise out of contingency. Initially, this seems like a wilful paradox designed to baffle but for Žižek its logic is capable of being allied with Lacanian thought to provide a powerful form of comprehension.

Circumstances exist, things happen in a causal nexus and a set of particulars account for a present moment. At a specific moment, for instance, a reader exists in a particular place at a precise time reading the previous sentence. It is obvious that countless events in the past – the different pasts in the lives of the reader and the writer, could have produced a different outcome. Given the moment that did transpire, the reading of a particular sentence by a particular person, it is equally obvious that a host of past events had to occur in the way they did in order for that specific moment to come about in the way it did. The conditions of possibility which existed and which happened to lead to that punctual moment were not all premeditated, there was a contingency at work, and it would be impossible to calculate the number of aleatory events that led to that moment existing precisely as it did. At the same time, though, in order to account for what happened in a rational way, these events can be retroactively positioned so as to produce a causal chain that makes the result appear inevitable. The event, the effect of contingency, can be accounted for by positing necessity as its cause. The contingency at the heart of the matter is occluded, allowing necessity to be posited as an organizing force. A part of the satisfaction that comes from watching a well-made film – Žižek's example is *Casablanca* because of the legend that different endings were played with during the course of filming – is that even if it ends in a way different from what was originally planned, we accept the ending that does occur as developing 'naturally' out of the preceding events: 'it is the ending that *retroactively* confers the consistency of an organic whole on the preceding events'.[31]

In this way, Žižek can state: 'It is therefore Necessity itself which depends on contingency.'[32] Such a chain of causal necessity implies an ontologically complete world but the utter contingency behind the moment of reading that particular sentence, the infinite possibilities that could have ensured such a moment never came into existence, insists on there being an ontologically confusing world.[33] Another way of putting this would be to say that order depends on chaos, the sense of there being a plan determining the outcome is an *après-coup* effect, and for Žižek this is what Hegel calls 'positing the presuppositions'.[34] This sense of opposites being brought together – contingency and necessity, order and chaos – lies at the heart of the Hegelian dialectic.

THE DIALECTIC

Hegel's dialectic has been traditionally presented in terms of three clear-cut stages: first there is a thesis, a proposition, an entity, whatever a thing is that enables rationality to recognize it as such; second, there is the antithesis, the positing of its negative, a moment of negation when its contradiction is encountered by reason; finally, there is a synthesis, a reconciliation via an overcoming, a sublation (*Aufhebung*), of the negation. Žižek is not the only modern scholar to object to this kind of triadic presentation and others have warned how no aspect of his philosophy is 'more interpreted, more misunderstood, and more controversial'[35] – but Žižek takes criticism of the traditional view to its limit and regards Hegel's 'absolute knowledge' not as a completion but its very opposite: the realization of a systematic failure inherent in any attempt to reach an omnipotent, neutrally positioned state of knowledge. 'Absolute knowledge' means taking on board, not disavowing, contradiction and antagonism as the kernel of every identity. The reconciliation, the synthesis, is the acknowledgement of division and the acceptance of the power of negativity driving the dialectic.[36]

As an account of Hegelian logic, what is misleading about a thesis/antithesis encounter leading to a synthesis is that it tends to set up the idea of two opposing forces as opposed to the idea of a split being reflected back into something's identity. What is meant here by the reflection of a split back into an identity is what follows from questioning the opposition between two terms – for example, law/transgression, no-violence/violence, essence/appearance, freedom/necessity, truth/error – and locating the opposition not where we initially take it to be. It seems at first that the asymmetry resides between the given term, the 'thesis' if one wishes to use this term, and its apparent opposite, the so-called 'antithesis'. What needs to be grasped, and this is the 'negation of the negation', is that the asymmetry lies *within* the second term; it is reflected back into it instead of just being there in the initial and stark opposition. Instead of the law, for example, being seen to be simply opposed by transgression, it is necessary to see the transgression as that which is necessary for the law to exist. A dialectical process accounts for the inversion of a crime, an illegitimate act of violence, into a necessary founding gesture, within the becoming that results in law. There is no law until an act of violence, a crime, made it possible; the status of the mythical always-existing law is something posited retroactively to make sense of the imposed rule of law. Similarly, an act that is defined as violent needs to be seen with reference to the larger systemic violence that imposes the standard which provides this very definition.[37] Or, to take a different example, the 'negation of the negation' in Proudhon's motto 'property is theft' is the shift from seeing theft as a deformation, a violation, of property to a dimension where theft is seen as built into the notion of property itself.[38] A fictional instance would be the way Darcy's pride in Jane Austen's novel only appears from within the vanity of Elizabeth and her prejudices.[39]

Aufhebung, the word used by Hegel to express what happens in the dialectical process, is an ordinary German word but with the double meaning of both abolishing and preserving. Hegel employs both meanings of the word and the doubling effect is there in Žižek's understanding of the dialectic as a process whereby what is overcome is a one-sidedness which is preserved when the negative assumes a positive identity.[40] Instead of a synthesis there is what Hegel terms a 'speculative' moment, an acknowledgement of a complicity of opposites in one identity. The split that gives rise to opposites is a fundamental one – as will shortly be seen, it is an ontological division – 'between Something and Nothing, between the One and the Void of its Place'.[41] This may well sound a bit too mystical for its own good but Chapter One of Hegel's *Science of Logic* can be looked at as an example of what has been said so far about the nature of the dialectic.

Seeking to avoid any presuppositions, Hegel starts *Science of Logic* not with something concrete like a chair or a mountain but with pure indeterminate being, just the thought of abstract, empty *being*. Thinking *is*. Instead of drawing any conclusions from this, like Descartes' *cogito ergo sum* (I think therefore I am), the focus remains on utterly minimalist, pure *being*, unspecified, without any characteristics other than the fact that being just *is*. What does conceiving of being in the abstract amount to when the ordinary way of conceiving of being, i.e. associating it with something other ('he is being stubborn', 'it is large and bulky'), is bracketed off? In Žižek's words:

Being is first posited as the subject (in the grammatical sense), and one endeavors to accord it some predicate, to determine it in any way possible. Yet every attempt fails: one cannot say anything determinate about Being: one cannot attribute to it any predicate, and thus Nothing qua the truth of Being functions as *a positivization, a 'substantialization,' of this impasse.*[42]

Nothing rather than something is the result of conceiving of being in the abstract – but with the proviso that thinking of nothing is still thinking. And, by the same token, thinking of being as nothing is still a thought of being, even if it is the simplicity of nothing, not the nothing of something particular but pure nothing.

Thinking of just empty *being* collapses, or doubles, into thinking of nothing; it becomes its opposite. Being and nothingness are *not*, ontologically speaking, two separate entities: nothing is being itself when viewed from a new perspective. The result is that to say what something is means saying what it is not: being is not nothing; nothing is not being. This doubling is a dynamic *becoming*, a combat that unifies being and nothing by undermining what would seem to be a clear and irreducible difference between the two and bringing them together in an incongruous tension.

One possible response to this account is to see it as an empty playing with words that makes nonsense of the laws of identity (a is a) and non-contradiction (a cannot be a and non-a). A different conclusion is that, thus far, difference is all; identity is inescapably bound up with difference, with its opposite, and unlike conventional, deductive logic the premise, in this case *being*, does not stay the same. Difference is not absolute, everything is in a state of change, of becoming between being and nothing. Changes of valency are immanent and the instability of becoming, for Hegel, arises from the intertwining of being and nothing; there is a passing over into an opposite state and, as Žižek puts it, 'it is wrong to say that the final Result "sublates" negativity by making it a subordinate moment of the concrete totality – the point is rather that the new positivity of the Result is nothing but positivized power of the Negative'.[43] What is seen as an impediment to the full progress of an identity is recognized as a necessary condition for its active existence in the first place.

Aufhebung results from a shift of perspective and not from a realization of what was always there, seed-like, waiting to evolve. What is already there is not a polarized duality but the entity's own negativity and the end point comes after 'the negation of the negation', with the realization of the nothingness inherent in what was formerly identified as a substantial positive. If this sounds all a little too rarefied for its own good, two of Žižek's examples help clarify the point being made: the title of Dickens' novel, *Great Expectations*, only properly realizes its notion when Pip upends the values he once held dear, cancelling out the negative connotations of his class consciousness by transforming them into a positive basis for communality and self-worth; Muhammad Ali became truly 'The

Greatest' not by victories in the ring but by overcoming the 'defeat' of Parkinson's disease and shakingly holding aloft the torch at the 1996 Olympic Games.[44] Both these cases show how the moment of negation involves a self-reflection, a reflection into its own agency of its lack, bringing the negation to an extreme so that it negates itself and becomes its opposite 'in the annihilation and retroactive restructuring of the presupposed contents'.[45]

Another classic real-world example that Žižek likes to evoke is the anti-Semite whose positive sense of identity is structured through and relies on the negative figure of the Jew; the anti-Semite's consistency of being would be undermined were it not for the Jew configured as a caustic force damaging social health. Žižek also likes to retell a Soviet joke about a Rabinovitch, a Jew who wishes to emigrate, to illustrate the dialectic. Rabinovitch tells an emigration official he has two reasons for wanting to emigrate, the first being his fear that the Soviet Union will collapse, Jews will be blamed and he will suffer in the pogroms that follow. When the official interrupts to state that he need not fear, the Soviet Union will last forever and Communists will never lose power, Rabinovitch replies that this indeed is his second reason. In terms of the Hegelian triad, the only difference between the synthesis and the antithesis 'lies in a certain turn through which what was a moment ago experienced as an obstacle, as an impediment, proves to be a positive condition'.[46]

One more example should be given because it concerns a term used in Hegel, the 'beautiful soul', that Žižek regularly uses to denounce the net effect of a certain political comportment. In *The Phenomenology of Spirit*, Hegel is discussing an ethical attitude that he calls 'conscience' and the dissemblance that pertains to one who invokes his conscientiousness as the only worthy criterion for a judgement being made of him.[47] The purity of his intentions are to be acknowledged but the agent reasons that the best way of maintaining integrity in the eyes of others is by not acting on the dictates of his conscience because his behaviour will be open to misinterpretation. He becomes a 'beautiful soul' and protects his purity by shunning active involvement in the world. The first movement here, the agent's conscientiousness that allows him to distance himself morally from action deemed ethically reprehensible, is a 'negation' but a further dialectical move brings the recognition that the agent needs to see himself as the passive victim of circumstances – and therefore needs those circumstances in place – in order to preserve the self-image of a pure heart:

> 'negation' is the Beautiful Soul's critical attitude towards its social surroundings, and the 'negation of negation' is the insight into how the Beautiful Soul itself depends on – and thus fully partici-pates in – the wicked universe it purports to reject.[48]

NEGATION

Every category of being carries its own negative within it, not intro-duced from an external source but as an immanent self-cancelling. A basic error regarding the traditional notion of the 'thesis' opposed by 'antithesis' is that it poses an initial plenum and thereby fails to recognize the inherent negation that rules out the possibility of there being any 'full immediacy' as a starting point[49]:

> the Hegelian subject – i.e., what Hegel designates as absolute, self-negativity – is nothing but the very gap which separates phenomena from the Thing, the abyss beyond phenomena conceived in its negative mode, i.e., the purely negative gesture of limiting phenomena without providing any positive content which would fill out the space beyond the limit.[50]

The notion of negation is absolutely central to Hegelian thought and it runs wholly counter to the synthesizing power of the mind elabo-rated by Kant. Integration is opposed by dismemberment and in one of Žižek's favourite quotations from Hegel, the state of negation is called the 'night of the world':

> The human being is this night, this empty nothing ... the interior of nature, that exists here – pure self – in phantasmagorical representations, is night all around, in which here shoots a bloody head – there another ghastly apparition, suddenly here before it, and just so disappears. One catches sight of this night when one looks human beings in the eye – into a night that becomes awful.[51]

Thus, for Žižek, the nature of the Lacanian subject is clear: when the imaginary and symbolic realms, constructed to gentrify this turbulent negativity, are subtracted from its existence, what remains is the subject. It is the state of absolute freedom that Schelling evoked in his account of the movement from Ground to Existence. The abyss of 'pure self' that Hegel refers to here is a stage in the dialectic but one that cannot, along the lines of the traditional interpretation of the triad, be reduced to 'a passing moment, sublated in the final result of the dialectical movement'. The 'synthesis', instead, is *'a form in which the radical negativity (the "night of the world") assumes determinate being'*.[52]

What Žižek is working towards here is a Hegelian version of the emergence of the symbolic order. He goes on to link the Lacanian notion of the symbolic as something 'dead' with Hegel's image, in the 'Preface' to the *Phenomenology of Spirit*, of death for the power of negation:

> ... detached from what circumscribes it, what is bound and is actual only in its context with others, should attain an existence of its own and a separate freedom – this is the tremendous power of the negative; it is the energy of thought, of the pure 'I'. Death, if that is what we want to call this non-actuality, is of all things the most dreadful ...[53]

Hegel employs this image of death for 'the energy of thought' that is capable of dissolving the apparently seamless fabric of reality, the 'circle that remains self-enclosed', bestowing autonomy on the parts which, before dismemberment, belonged to an organic whole.[54] The context for this quotation from the *'Preface'* is Hegel's praise for the power of reason and this capacity is correlated by Žižek with Lacan's depiction of the symbolic and the big Other as a constraining and containing network of signifiers: 'The power of understanding consists in this capacity to reduce the organic whole of experience to an appendix to the "dead" symbolic classification.'[55] The big Other may be a system of 'dead' symbolic fictions but this negativity assumes a positive form when the big Other weaves a stable fabric out of such fictions, a sociocultural fabric that holds together a community of heteronomous individuals.

Going back to the emergence of the symbolic from Hegel's description of the nocturnal unruliness, Žižek's concern is with the dysfunctionality at the heart of matter that produces such a traumatic disturbance that the symbolic is produced in order to heal this wound, to domesticate a turbulence that cannot otherwise be contained.[56] Negativity, however, remains inherent to the symbolic order and, by way of bringing Hegel and Lacan together, negativity equates with the death drive as that which is inherently disruptive within the psyche. Recognizing the immanent nature of the negative is, for Žižek, the recognition of this movement from the 'night of the world' to the symbolic and the way in which the positive can be seen as a materialization of the negative. Such a self-recognition is what, in *Phenomenology of Spirit*, Hegel refers to as the power of 'looking the negative in the face, and tarrying with it'.[57]

What then is the state of 'absolute knowledge' to which Hegel's thought is said to aspire and finally obtain?

'ABSOLUTE KNOWLEDGE'

Hegel's *Phenomenology of Spirit* as a body of thought works towards a final state of 'absolute knowledge' on the part of 'absolute Spirit' but what does this final state amount to? As a way of answering this, it is worth looking at how *Phenomenology of Spirit* gets underway with its opening examination of sense-certainty as a basis for knowledge, an examination which Žižek labels 'the elementary Hegelian procedure'.[58]

What a thing is first taken to be, 'in itself', would seem to be revealed intuitively by our senses: by focusing our attention on something, a tree or a house for instance, the pure, unfiltered immediacy of the experience – *this* is spatially *here*, temporally *now* – would suggest that one is immediately and directly acquainted with a truth without any need for mediation. Or so it seems. The problem is that the certainty, something that can be shared by others, is only a certainty of a universal *this, here, now* and not a certainty about the particularity of the object itself:

> Here is, e.g., the tree. If I turn around, this truth has vanished and is converted into its opposite: no tree is here, but a house instead. 'Here' itself does not vanish; on the contrary, it abides constant in the vanishing of the house, the tree, etc., and is indifferently house or tree.[59]

Despite the unique particularity of the moment, no word is confided to the subject that captures and expresses the absolute truth of this undeviating instant.

We can try to pin down a specificity and thereby rescue the validity of our sense-certainty by insisting on the singularity not of the object but of the 'I' whose sense uniquely intuits the thing: 'The force of its truth thus lies now in the "I", in the immediacy of *my seeing, hearing*'.[60] Again, though, there is no determinacy to this because my 'I' cannot be distinguished from anyone else's 'I'; reporting a sensuous certainty because it is mine and not yours only repeats the empty universal form common to everyone's 'I'; it fails to capture any essence or 'thisness' of the object. Even if we focus intensely and exclusively on our private sensual moment and point to our punctual certainty the moment will be in the past as soon as we point to it.

Hegel's procedure here is to show how the insufficiency of our initial certainty discloses itself from within when we distinguish more closely between what is being said or experienced from what was meant to be the case. In this way, a complexity replaces what was first deemed a straightforward truth and an incompleteness emerges from what was first taken as indubitably complete. A power of negativity is introduced when, in the case of sense certainty, a self-enclosed moment is sundered and a rift introduced between what is said (which fails to capture the solipsistic moment of sense-certainty) and what is meant (the 'truth' of the solipsistic moment itself). For Žižek, 'the dialectical movement is activated by the discord between what consciousness "means to say" and what it effectively says' and Hegel 'perceives it as the Spirit's supreme achievement ... to disengage itself from the immediacy of what is simply given, to break up its organic unity'.[61]

The attainment of this disengagement is not, however, part of a teleological movement towards some final order. The case for sense-certainty as the basis for knowledge is the first stage in Hegel's procedure of demonstrating how we fail in our purpose because of the way we approach the world, attributing a wholeness to ideas which prove to be limited and incomplete. This procedure continues with other adopted standpoints of consciousness, self-consciousness, reason, morality and religion, showing, argues Hegel, how they are all one-sided: 'by themselves they are single and separate ... Our *own* act here has been simply to *gather together* the separate moments, each of which in principle exhibits the life of Spirit in its entirety.' This is far less than some all-encompassing knowledge, some supreme signification, and for many readers approaching Hegel through the traditional lens as the great totalizer the conclusion of the *Phenomenology of Spirit* can seem frustratingly brief and anti-climactic. For Žižek, this lack of closure is the key to its virtue:

> ... its final outcome ('absolute knowledge') does not bring about a found harmony but rather entails a kind of reflective inversion: it confronts the subject with the fact that *the true Absolute is nothing but the logical disposition of its previous failed attempts to conceive the Absolute* – that is, with the vertiginous experience that Truth itself coincides with the path towards Truth.[62]

The search for epistemological certitude only comes to an end when it is realized that knowledge *is* the working through of errors and grasping how they make up the entirety that was being sought. What matters is the transformation, the passage of negativity. Hegel's Absolute is what was said above about the 'the negation of the negation' being the realization of the nothingness inherent in what was formerly identified as a substantial positive. Absolute knowledge is the Hegelian Spirit's full awareness of its rapture in the movement of becoming between being and nothing; and the *Phenomenology of Spirit* is the journey of consciousness from one set of master signifiers to another, each form breaking down under the restless sway of the negative.

Reaching the Absolute means reaching a point where it can be seen that there is no transcendent position, no supersensible noumenal order, a situation deftly expressed by Jonathan Rée when describing how the '*Phenomenology* is not the biography of absolute knowledge, but its collective autobiography: the confessions of a penitent dogmatist who lives within us all'.[63] One of the most important dogmas that needs to be shed is that of a complete reality, a full essence, that invisibly constitutes the ontological ground-zero upon which the ephemeral world of appearance is built. This, for Žižek, is a crucial difference between Kant and Hegel.

APPEARANCE IS REALITY

It has been said already how for Žižek the importance of Kant is that his transcendental turn makes possible a conclusion that he himself never arrived at; an example of this is the way in which we relate to experiential reality:

Phenomenal reality is not simply the way things appear to me. It designates the way things 'really' appear to me, the way they constitute phenomenal reality, as opposed to a mere subjective/ illusory appearance. Consequently, when I misperceive some object in my phenomenal reality, when I mistake it for a different object, what is wrong is not that I am unaware of how 'things really are in themselves' but of how they 'really appear' to me. One cannot overestimate the importance of this Kantian turn.[64]

Schelling and Hegel, as if sensing this truth as something in Kant more than was in Kant himself, both regard the noumenal Thing-in-itself as a construction of thought and, agreeing with this, Žižek emphasizes how this does not entail an extreme idealism: 'Hegel's point is not a delirious solipsism, but rather a simple insight into how we – finite, historical subjects – forever lack any measuring-rod which would guarantee our contact with the Thing itself.'[65] This same insight lies behind Žižek's remark quoted at the start of this chapter about there being no mind outside of reality. We cannot establish the existence of the noumenal because to do so would be to step outside of our world and knowledgeably experience what is taken to exist, the noumenal that is, but which must lie beyond our ken.[66] Although the context is a quite different one, the same underlying point is made in *The Pervert's Guide to the Cinema* when Žižek, referring to *The Matrix*, speaks of wanting the 'third pill', the one that makes him 'see not the reality behind the illusion but the reality in illusion itself'.[67]

We regard appearances as necessarily masking some deeper, inaccessible reality and so we posit the noumenal:

> The inner world, or supersensible beyond, has, however, *come into being*: it *comes from* the world of appearance which has mediated it: in other words, appearance is its essence and, in fact, its filling. The supersensible is the sensuous and the perceived posited as it is *in truth*; but the *truth* of the sensuous and the perceived is to be *appearances*. The supersensible is therefore *appearances qua appearances*.[68]

What Hegel is saying here is explained by Žižek in dialectical parlance, locating the opposition between essence and appearance *within* the second term:

We should always bear in mind that, in Hegel's dialectic of appearance and essence, it is appearance which is the asymmetrical encompassing term: the difference between essence and appearance is internal to appearance, *not* to essence ... with regard to the opposition essence/appearance, immediate 'reality' is on the side of appearance.[69]

It is a question of presentation, not representation. There is, in other words, no essence that precedes appearance; no essence that manifests itself in appearance, only the illusion of such an essence. The need that is felt for the noumenal is the essence reflected in the self-fissure, the split, that attaches itself to appearance.[70] Unpacking this point of view takes one to the heart of Žižek's ontology and the Hegelian statement that Substance is Subject.

ŽIŽEK'S ONTOLOGY

At this stage it seems reasonable to pose the question put by an anti-Hegelian:

What reason can be assigned for this alleged desire on the part of being to negate itself and to not know itself? Why ... should it make this mad effort to annul itself? For Hegel's system does nothing less than make being go mad, and introduce madness into all things.[71]

A response to this question brings one back to Schelling and the origins of human history in the passage from nature to culture and the birth of consciousness. As seen, Žižek finds in Schelling a perceptive account of subjectivity emerging from a moment of contraction, a withdrawal from reality that can be characterized as a necessary journey through madness. Hegel's 'night of the world' describes this same moment. What Schelling and Hegel have in common for Žižek is an account of how the symbolic order can be seen as the construction of a substitute formation for what came before the night of the world. This earlier state, a Real that can be understood on one level in terms of the animal's unreflecting immersion in its life-world,[72] has to be annulled in order to create the possibility of human commitment to the symbolic.

At some stage in human evolution there occurred a fissure that resulted in an antagonism between instinctual nature and an ungovernable excess, the libidinal inconsistency called the death drive that reaches down to the ontological level of human nature. This antagonism can also be associated with the failure of the symbolic to endow the subject with a complete identity, a failure that is unavoidable given the ontological void out of which subjectivity emerges. This failure is behind the drive's redemptive impulse to fasten onto those *objets petit a* that hold out the promise of a final self-enclosure, albeit a consummation that remains perpetually out of reach. At the level of Hegelian thought, and this is the synthesis that Žižek seeks to achieve between Lacan and German idealism, this death drive is negativity.[73] Psychoanalytically, this negativity has to be repressed in the passage from the pre-symbolic state of 'nature' to that of 'culture' and it accounts for that in-between stage, Žižek's 'vanishing mediator' and Hegel's 'night of the world', that undermines any notion of a smooth evolutionary progression from pre-lingual animal to human.[74] The subject is defined by this gap and can never be properly at home in its environment, an alienated state evoked by the discrepancy between the figure of the woman and the strangely unreal background in da Vinci's *Mona Lisa* or by Hitchcock's use of scenes where the actors perform against an obviously projected background.[75]

It is possible now to return to the ambivalence that was noted earlier in Žižek's employment of the concept of the Real. He links Hegel and Lacan because in their different ways they share an awareness of the disjunction between ordinary lived reality and the void of the Real: 'What we forget when we pursue our daily life is that our human universe is nothing but an embodiment of the radically inhuman "abstract negativity" of the abyss we experience when we face the "night of the world".'[76] Kant is seen to have displaced this negativity by locating it in the untravellable space between the subject's experience of phenomena and the thing in itself whereas Hegel positions negativity within the thing itself, making it an inescapable part of our experience. What for Kant was an issue of epistemology – the finite knowledge of the subject, the unknowable dominion of the noumenal – is transformed by Hegel into an ontological concern with the Real, with being as punctured and fissured by division and gaps.

The antinomies drawn up by Kant established a position beyond which reason should not tread but Hegel, following Fichte and

Schelling, dismantled the cognitive fence separating the noumenal from the phenomenal by locating the contradictions that gave rise to Kant's antinomies within the conceptual field itself. The antinomies that were contained within the boundaries of the subject's thinking are now seen as irreducible, fracturing elements of the Real:

> All Hegel does is, in a way, to supplement Kant's well-known motto of the transcendental constitution of reality ('the conditions of possibility of our knowledge are at the same time the conditions of possibility of the object of our knowledge') by its negative – the limitation of our knowledge (its failure to grasp the whole of being, the way our knowledge gets inexorably entangled in contradictions and inconsistencies) is simultaneously the limitation of the very object of our knowledge, that is, the gaps and voids in our knowledge of reality are simultaneously the gaps and voids in the 'real' ontological edifice itself.[77]

Žižek finds the place for Lacan in Hegel by seeing the Real as the correlate of the self-division and self-doubling within phenomena; the Real surfaces when the dialectical movement that is a shift of perspective arising from the innate inconsistency of being makes itself felt. This fundamental inconsistency is, by way of one response to the question posed at the start, precisely what makes being 'go mad'. At the epistemological level, there is inherent in the status of every concept or category that seeks a determinate grip on reality a self-bifurcation. Attempts to establish a grip on the hyperactive flux of being are necessary if we are to conceive of reality but it is also an impossible endeavour because 'the moment we fully and consequently "apply" it to reality, it disintegrates and/or turns into its opposite'.[78]

The Real is not like Kant's 'thing-in-itself', the genuine essence that cannot be directly accessed; the Real is the void, the gap, that separates one perspective from another. Without the Real, there is no self-doubling, no dialectic. For both Hegel and Lacan, reality is inconsistent, non-homogeneous, and Žižek takes on board the full philosophical force of 'unfinished reality', illustrating it cinematically with the scene from *Alien Resurrection* when the cloned Ripley encounters the failed versions of herself.[79] Given that reality is ontologically incomplete, unsutured, not coincident with itself, it necessarily follows that our proper understanding of the world must be bound up with and reflect this fact:

> This is why, if we are to grasp the core of Hegel's dialectical process properly, we have to overcome the opposition between dialectics as an ontological process (taking place in the 'thing itself') and dialectics as an epistemological process (revealing the movement of our cognition of reality). The dialectical process is 'epistemological'; it reveals the shifts of perspective in our conceiving/grasping reality; however, *these shifts, at the same time, concern the 'thing itself'*.[80]

In his later work Žižek explains this ontology through the idea of parallax, the difference in the position of an object caused by a change in the position of the point of observation. The insurmountable gap of parallax is a way of picturing the Hegelian insight that reality 'is caught in the movement of our knowing it'.[81] Given this correspondence between the ontological and the epistemological, it follows that there cannot be any final state of knowledge arising from a complete picture of a complete world. What also follows from this correspondence is a more complex understanding of the Lacanian Real, a parallax real: when the subject, ordinarily ensconced within the imaginary-symbolic matrix, is disturbed sufficiently enough to come close to a point of contact with the fissured, self-refuting ground of reality then, and only then, is there a sense of touching the Real. But there is nothing tangible waiting there to be touched: 'the status of the Real is purely parallactic and, as such, non-substantial: it has no substantial density in itself, it is just a gap between two points of perspective, perceptible only in the shift from the one to the other'.[82]

At the same time, though, the Real cannot be reduced to just a retrospectively constructed fiction within the symbolic. In order for it to be experienced there must be something there causing this experience and it is not pure illusion. The correspondence that exists between the epistemological and the ontological is one defined by a shared dysfunctionality; the self-refuting nature of the dialectical process mirrors the inconsistency of the world itself and in this sense it is 'the ultimate proof that our thought is not merely a logical game we play, but is able to reach reality itself, expressing its inherent structuring principle'.[83] There are deadlocks and impasses such as Kant's antinomies that are immanent to the symbolic order and they register as an aspect of the foreclosed Real over which the imaginary and symbolic appear as palimpsestic layers. In case this seems like a relapse into thinking of the Real as a proto-reality, the 'really real', it needs re-emphasizing that the division between the noumenal and the phenomenal is one produced, dialectically, within the phenomenal. To think otherwise, to conceive of some raw matter underlying everything, argues Žižek, leads to one or other kind of spirituality 'as in Tarkovsky's *Solaris*, in which the dense plastic matter of the planet directly embodies Mind'; a proper materialism, on the other hand, thinks in 'constellations in which matter seems to "disappear," like the pure oscillations of the superstrings or quantum vibrations ... the fact that there is only void'.[84] Ultimately, and this has to be taken on board if Žižek's real is not held to be riddled with contradiction, there is an 'unfathomable X'.[85] The night of the world, negativity, death drive, is the hyper-flux of being, a surplus that can spill over and cause a temporary malfunction in the symbolic. A way of putting this would be to say that the excess of being can overwhelm the resources of our mediated reality and the Real is the experience of this haemorrhaging. Also, however, because it is an excess that dialectically splits and sublates being, the Real is at the same time what prevents us accessing it:

> The Real is ... *simultaneously* the Thing to which direct access is not possible and the obstacle that prevents this direct access; the Thing that eludes our grasp and the distorting screen that makes us miss the Thing.[86]

Another way of approaching this ontology is by way of an enigmatic statement from *Phenomenology of Spirit* that Žižek likes to refer to: 'the *being of Spirit is a bone*'.[87] It seems an absurd contradiction to reduce the richly mutable arena of subjectivity (spirit) to an inert material object (bone) but, argues Žižek, it is the very negativity of this contradiction, the disturbing incompatibility expressed by the statement, that makes up the nature of subjectivity. This is another of those 'speculative' moments, a coming together of two apparently contradictory terms, because of the way we '*succeed* in transmitting the dimension of subjectivity *by means of the failure itself*'.[88] There is no signifier that can properly represent the subject, and phrenology (measuring the cranial bone as an indicator of the individual's personality), like *objet petit a*, provides a way of filling out the void by objectifying the lack that defines the subject. Žižek is able to interpret Hegel's statement as German idealism's version of the Lacanian formula of fantasy, $ ◊ a, because the absurdity of equating spirit with bone captures the absurd hope that the barred subject is not empty, is not something more substantial than the fantasy that sustains it. It is only in the irreducible gap between the subject's fantasmic identifications and its empty self that the subject truly emerges and so, in parallel with the truth behind the spirit-is-a-bone statement, Žižek can state how 'the subject is strictly correlative to its own impossibility; its limit is its positive condition'.[89]

SUBSTANCE AS SUBJECT

An idea contained in another enigmatic remark from *Phenomenology of Spirit* – 'everything turns on grasping and expressing the True, not only as *Substance* but equally as *Subject*'[90] – becomes central to Žižek's philosophy and it follows on from the alignment traced between the ontological and the epistemological in Hegel's dialectic. It has been seen how the idea of the subject as an external observer of the world has to be qualified because of the way the subject is a part of the natural, material foundation, (substance) which is reflected upon. Given that reality itself is inconsistent and incomplete and given that there is no place where the mind can position itself outside of or above the reality of which it is a part, there is, then, a crucial entailment: what is taken to be the external reflection (the subject observing the world) has to be reflected back as an internal counterpart (the observing subject is part of the world). Kant maintains a separation between subject (the transcendental set of categories making experience possible) and substance (the Thing-in-itself) 'whereas Hegel endeavours to grasp Substance itself as Subject ... our act of knowledge is included in advance in its substantial content'.[91] This is one way of drawing the irrevocable dividing line between Kant and Hegel:

> Kant's vision is meaningless and inconsistent, since [by the existence of the Thing-in-itself] it secretly reintroduces the ontologically fully constituted divine totality, i.e. a world conceived only as substance, not also as subject.[92]

Žižek seeks to clarify this point, the identity of substance with subject, by pointing to the ontological weight that can adhere to the everyday way of describing a point of view that is partial as 'subjective'. When such a weighting is given to the 'subjective' it follows that 'non-truth, error, is inherent to Truth itself' and, conversely, 'their non-identity (the gap separating the Subject from the Substance) is strictly correlative to the inherent non-identity, split, of the Substance itself'.[93] Žižek is saying here that the ground of identity, what the subject and substance have in common, is a non-identity that is internal to each. It is the haemorrhaging of being in the world that makes reality in its perpetual openness incomplete and this is as necessarily true of subject as it is of substance.

Žižek describes how the Real '*qua* traumatic antagonism is, as it were, the objective factor of *subjectivization* itself; it is the object which accounts for the failure of every neutral-objective representation, the object which "pathologizes" the subject's gaze or approach, makes it biased, pulls it askew'.[94] What is meant here by the 'objective factor of *subjectivization*' is illustrated by way of Heisenberg's uncertainty principle and Žižek's rejection of any Kantian interpretation of this principle along the lines of the inescapable effect of the observer on the observed or the impossibility of ever reaching the thing-in-itself. The failure to determine a particle's position and momentum *at the same time* reflects the nature of the system itself; indeed, neither position or momentum exist *until* measured by an observer.[95] The observing subject is part of the substance, it is 'inscribed' into it ontologically, and in this sense one part of substance is looking at another part and thereby objectifying itself.[96] The gaze of the subject is, in Hegelian parlance, reflected back into the substance. As Adrian Johnston headily expresses it:

> Each individual consciousness really is the natural material universe staring back at itself through the eyes of something immeasurably smaller in relation to it than a grain of sand: the human gaze actually is the universe gazing upon itself in and through a finite part of itself.[97]

It is necessary to think of the subject in Žižek's ontology not in terms of an 'I', a self-aware, bodily agent, but as the place within substance '*that sustains the very ontological order of being*'.[98] This notion is difficult to grasp because it involves the idea of an element of substance acquiring for itself a subjectification: ' "subject" is nothing but the name for this inner distance of "substance" towards itself, the name for this empty place from which the substance can perceive itself as something "alien"'.[99] The subject here is not to be thought of as an individual possessing its own rich interiority but as the experience of the negation, the restlessness, at the heart of substance. The journey from substance to this subject is what is represented by Hegel in his description of the 'night of the world' passage quoted above; there is a negativity within the substance of human nature and out of this abyss the subject, and language, emerges; the pure self which, states Hegel, 'must enter into existence, become an object, oppose itself to this innerness to be external; return to being. This is language as name-giving power'.[100]

Part of the difficulty in comprehending this archaeology of being is that Žižek is grappling with the task of providing a phylogenetic account, a macrocosmic picture, which accounts materially for the subject without falling into an idealism that solipsistically relies on a mind-dependent reality. This task involves an account of human evolution that, as mentioned above (p. 58), sees consciousness emerging as the result of something going wrong, a biological glitch for which cognitivism cannot offer a satisfactory explanation but which can be understood in terms of Hegelian negativity and the Freudian–Lacanian death drive. Consciousness results from an evolutionary short circuiting that permits one natural element to acquire a distance from itself: 'the constitutive gesture of subjectivity is a violent reversal of the preceding "natural" substantial balance – the "subject" is some subordinated moment of the presupposed substantial totality that ... elevates itself into the Master of its own Ground'.[101] The 'reversal' being described here, a primordial unrest within being, is, he goes on to say, the dialectical conduit in which Substance becomes Subject.

There is another important dimension to the idea of substance as subject that serves to introduce Žižek's political philosophy. The Kantian things-in-themselves belong to an inaccessible noumenal order which is consistent within itself, substance without subject, and this is to be contrasted with a Hegelian–Lacanian picture of reality as 'not-all', where substance and subject are equally inter-nally fractured. For Kant, freedom is only possible within the noumenal order of being; for Žižek, 'noumenal Freedom' is only possible because of a 'not-all' universe, it is *nothing but* a rupture within phenomenal reality'.[102] What Žižek means by this can be seen by returning to the contingency/necessity paradox from the beginning of this chapter and the way in which it creates a space for a narrative to be produced which transforms the contingent into the necessary. What is allowed for is a choice of how we symbolize and make sense of what happens – fate, destiny, an adamantine causal chain, an ideology, are some of the possibilities – and this choice is itself contingent. What happens (substance) is open to us (subject) to symbolize: 'freedom is ... the (contingent) choice of the modality by means of which we symbolize the contingent real or impose some narrative necessity upon it'.[103] This point about the confluence of necessity and contingency, by the way, also illustrates the nature of the Hegelian dialectic. The synthesis of the two terms cannot be reduced to a moment of *Aufhebung*, the sublation of contingency in some larger, overall moment of necessity, because the split between chance (freedom) and necessity is reflected back into the identity of whatever mode we choose to homogenize and make sense of the flux:

> If, for example, we are Marxists, the entire past is perceived as a long narrative whose constant theme is the class struggle ... if we are liberals, the past tells the story of the gradual emancipation of the individual from the constraints of collectivity and Fate, and so on. And it is *here* that freedom and the subject intervene: freedom is *stricto sensu* the contingency of necessity – that is, it is contained in the initial 'if ...', in the (contingent) choice of the modality by means of which we symbolize the contingent real or impose some narrative necessity upon it. 'Substance as subject' means that the very necessity that sublates contingency by positing it as its ideal moment is itself contingent.[104]

CHAPTER FOUR

ŽIŽEK AND COMMUNISM

Žižek's Marxism is not of the catechismal kind and a development in his attitude towards it can be traced from his early to more recent writings. In his first book in English, *The Sublime Object Of Ideology* (1989), Marxism is only one expression of the antagonism that underlies society, one way of symbolizing and 'quilting' reality, but two years later in *They Know Not What They Do*, while class struggle is not the supreme meaning for every aspect of the social whole it is fundamental. Class struggle explains why there is no rational totality – it is the rift, the impediment blocking any final harmony – and social reality is understandable in the way its sets about trying to integrate the antagonism that structures it in the first place. In the Lacanian sense, he says, class struggle belongs to the *'real'* because it produces an effect 'which exists only in order to efface the causes of its existence'.[1] By 2010, class conflict as the undertow shaping the course of our lives is a given; it is the real of our socio-economic existence but, crucially, it is also capable of being changed:

Today, the ruling ideology endeavours to make us accept the 'impossibility' of radical change, of abolishing capitalism, of a democracy not reduced to a corrupt parliamentary game, in order to render invisible the impossible-real of the antagonism that cuts across capitalist societies. This real is 'impossible' in the sense that it is the impossible of the existing social order, its constitutive antagonism; which is not to imply that this impossible-real cannot be directly dealt with, or radically transformed.[2]

The antagonism being referred to here is class struggle and, as seen from his approach to ideology (p. 43), class conflict informs the application of Žižek's theoretical concerns to social and political life. Is it possible, though, that the very efficacy of such a psycho-analytic approach, relying as it seems to do on more or less invariant features of the human condition, acts as a brake on his and any emancipatory political project that seeks to replace capitalism as a socioeconomic system?

The communist ideal in traditional Marxism is an order that fully releases productive potentiality, unchaining it from the inherent contradictions in capitalism which thwart a smooth and progressive release of productive forces. For Žižek, aware of the irony, this is a fantasy internal to capitalism itself; a fantasy premised on ignoring the requirement of capitalism's dynamic for a fundamental obstacle to be in place for its own effective functioning to proceed.[3] The argument for saying this is that the compulsive consumption endemic to capitalism arises from meeting a need for surplus enjoyment and it is this that fuels the profit-seeking motor of the socio-economic system. This profit-seeking, manifested in the Marxian concept of surplus value, depends on the obstacle of the divided subject's *jouissance*. This substance of human life is there in the unconscious as an ahistorical, self-alienating kernel and capitalism thrives on it.

What is meant here by surplus enjoyment? Žižek uses the soft drink Coca-Cola as an example because of the way it is enjoyed not primarily to quench thirst, which would be sufficient to satisfy the need of a non-surplus enjoyment, but because it offers something extra, some elusive X which will meet a need irreducible to a concrete requirement like the quenching of thirst.[4] A commodity that can market itself with subliminal force will create a paradigmatic level of surplus value because it is seen to render back something perceived to be lost, the Lacanian *objet petit a*: 'the excess of capitalist consumption always functions as the reaction to a fundamental lack'.[5] There is, in other words, a libidinal economy at work within the free-market economy and this is what accounts for the link between surplus enjoyment and surplus value. The manufacturing of commodities that promise to satisfy wants, in the way that Coca-Cola does, instates the subject's psychical lack within cycles of consumption. At a macroeconomic level, money is invested in commodities in order to sell them again and make a profit and, arising out of this circulation, 'capital becomes an end in itself, for the expansion of value takes place only within this constantly renewed movement. The circulation of capital has therefore no limits'. Žižek quotes these words from *Capital* as an instance of 'the mode of drive' that 'inheres to capitalism' and which 'propels the whole capitalist machinery'.[6] Marx identified the frenzied tune that the dynamic of productivity dances to but failed to recognize how this frenzy is the very antagonism, the contradiction, that drives capitalism; removing the antagonism does not simply lead to a communist idyll that enhances the productive drive: 'if we abolish the obstacle, the inherent contradiction of capitalism, we do not get the fully unleashed drive to productivity, we lose precisely this productivity that seemed to be generated and simultaneously thwarted by capitalism'; the system 'parasitizes on and exploits the pure drive of Life'.[7]

A related aspect here is Žižek's account of the fetish as the embodiment of something disavowed and thereby of assistance in the task of coping with a difficulty.

So, when we are bombarded by claims that in our post-ideological cynical era nobody believes in the proclaimed ideals, when we encounter a person who claims he is cured of any beliefs, accepting social reality the way it really is, one should always counter such claims with the question: OK, but *where is the fetish which enables you to (pretend to) accept reality 'the way it really is'?*[8]

Money is such fetish both at a personal level, helping to account for the many strange and 'irrational' ways it influences behaviour, and at a structural level through its functioning as the means for the circulation of commodities. The limitless drive to accumulate capital is bound up with the way money functions as the sublime fetish-object of the capitalist world we inhabit, an idea made explicit in Marx but which Žižek traces back to a notion in Schelling's of the materialization of the spirit.[9] We behave towards money as if it possessed some non-material quality and disavow, like the true fetishist, our knowledge that this is not the case. It is a sublime object because it is seen to transcend the corporeal, fulfilling the way fetishism dispenses with the difference between *objet petit a* and the cause of desire, turning the cause directly into the object of desire.[10]

If the Lacanian ideas that Žižek applies so fruitfully to everyday life are based on fundamental notions of a less-than-harmonious human constitution and if capitalism taps deeply into the libidinal source of this imbalance, does this not buttress the resigned conservative's axiom that human nature dictates the inevitable failure of any communist-inspired politics, as amply demonstrated by the history of the Soviet Union? Capitalism, warts and all, succeeds because aspects of human nature render alternative economic systems hopeless failures by comparison. To state it baldly, is there an inherent problem in trying to reconcile Lacan with Marx? The terms of Žižek's refusal to accept this argument can be seen in the way, within Lacanian thought, he seeks to move beyond the point which fixes on a 'quasi-transcendental reading ... focused on the notion of the Real as the impossible Thing-in-itself'.[11] The early Žižek sometimes encourages such a reading, allowing for the Real to become a barrier, behind which the disempowered subject is corralled within the symbolic and in thrall to the big Other. The Real is not some definitive referent that frames and confines the play of the symbolic; it is, instead, the traumatic antagonism that thwarts any possibility of representing external reality as symbolically neutral.

Žižek's later use of the idea of parallax is used to locate the Real in a way that is consonant with seeing it as the traumatic antagonism. Lacking the density that is part of any substance, the Real becomes the gap that is discernible in the shift from one point of observation to another. An explicit contrast is drawn between this and the 'standard (Lacanian) register of the Real as that which "always returns to its place" – as that which remains the same in all possible (symbolic) universes'.[12]

To say that something remains the same is not identical to saying something is always there. This might look like a semantic quibble but Žižek does not think so and tremendous significance is attached to making clear the nature of the distinction. One approach to this difference is to draw a line between 'evolutionary historicism', a reductionism that sees everything as purely historical, and 'historicity proper' which:

> involves a dialectical relationship to some unhistorical kernel that stays the same – not as an underlying Essence but as a rock that trips up every attempt to integrate it into the symbolic order. This rock is the Thing *qua* 'the part of the Real that suffers from the signifier' (Lacan) – the real 'suffers' in so far as it is the trauma that cannot be properly articulated in the signifying chain.[13]

Everything has an historical context but some things can be trans-historical (like the statement that everything has an historical context) and this allows for the dialectical relationship between change and permanence being acknowledged here. This helps explain why Žižek likes to refer to Benjamin's 'Theses on the Philosophy of History' and the idea of the present realizing and redeeming a possibility that was foreclosed in the past.[14] It is how we understand and interpret the past that determines how it determines us. In Žižek's words:

> In the revolutionary explosion, another utopian dimension shines through, that of universal emancipation, which is in fact the 'excess' betrayed by the market reality that takes over on the morning after. This excess is not simply abolished or dismissed as irrelevant, but is, as it were, transposed into the virtual state, as a dream waiting to be realised.[15]

The past is not just what happened before the present; there is an unpredictability to it and instead of modelling the Real as a hard, unchangeable core, it is more aptly representable as a site of perpetual strife, an arena of the virtual that, retrospectively, assumes a fictional identity. Žižek illustrates what is meant here by considering how two people in love may feel as if what binds them together is thwarted only by present conditions and that if circumstances were different, 'another time, another place', their love would be properly fulfilled. While it may seem brutal but realistic to puncture the fantasy and insist there is no Other place, another response would be to say: 'No: the "Real as impossible" means here that THE IMPOSSIBLE DOES HAPPEN, that "miracles" like Love (or political revolution: "in some respects, a revolution is a miracle," Lenin said in 1921) DO occur'.[16] The lovers can assert the truth of their subjective position without recourse to fantasy.

Working towards a fictional identity that is less damaging to the community of a body politic than capitalism – and communism is the name for such a viable alternative – has for Žižek a character that unites Hegelian and psychoanalytic ideas. It can be called dialectical materialism, notwithstanding the forbiddingly gloomy connotations the term invites, and approached through the Lacanian notion of the act. Just as the lovers above can assert a truth in the face of contingency the politically aware can perform a similarly meaningful gesture at the level of a symbolic act, like the miners' band in the strike of 1984–1985 in the film *Brassed Off* who after their defeat go on playing to enshrine the legitimacy of their struggle and to state who they are.[17] If the miners' strike had been successful, their victory might have been an act in the proper and full sense, not a symbolic statement of their identity but, given the possible political repercussions of defeating Thatcher, a serious undermining of the prevailing symbolic order. The idea of an act, then, carries a heavy theoretical punch because of the political force behind it.

THE ACT

The act, a term developed by Žižek from Lacan, is transgressive and disruptive of the symbolic order, something unanticipated by the subject involved who only comes retrospectively to an awareness of what has occurred. An act ruptures the subject's disavowed attachment to the status quo, the unconscious source of which underpins capitalism's ideological grip on the subject.

Žižek equates acts with the dimension of the 'divine' in human affairs and an act, if disavowed, reveals a person's ethical betrayal.[18] The unpredictability of an act is, for Žižek, a way of escaping from the closed teleology of traditional Marxism, with its belief in the inevitability of capitalism's collapse through internal contradictions, without sacrificing a belief in the possibility of fundamental change. While he finds no comfort in the oracular 'truths' of Marxism – Žižek did not, for example, detect capitalism's death throes in the global financial crisis of 2008, seeing instead that it would only make the system stronger[19] – there is hope in the act:

> An act is more than an intervention into the domain of the possible – an act changes the very coordinates of what is possible and thus retroactively creates its own conditions of possibility. This is why communism also concerns the real: to act as a communist means to intervene into the real of the basic antagonism which underlies today's global capitalism.[20]

The only alternative to entering the symbolic order is psychosis but the act is a reliving of the possibility of a choice, an opening up of something 'before' or 'outside' the symbolic order. Lacan's term for the psychoanalytic cure, traversing the fantasy, becomes for Žižek a disturbance of the symbolic order by an act that suspends the support the order receives at a psychical level. What we should attend to and be mindful of is a knowledge of the self without any *objet petit a* (the wisdom attested to by the old tortoise in the film *Kung Fu Panda*[21]). An act which traverses the fantasy is necessarily traumatic because it fundamentally estranges the subject:

> If there is a subject to the act, it is not the subject of subjectivization, of integration and recognition, of assuming the act as 'my own', but, rather, an uncanny 'acephalous' subject through which the act takes place as that which is 'in him more than himself.[22]

This all sounds very far removed from political life as we know it but the conditions for revolutionary change are being adumbrated and Žižek's feet are firmly on the ground even though his elevated language sometimes strains towards the abstruse. He wants to stress how effecting a change to the political order of capitalism requires a disruption to the symbolic order, a breaking down of the existing horizons of meaning, and while this can be translated into concrete political action it will only do so effectively if the libidinal economy of the big Other is undermined and the ideology supporting the existing order destabilized. Žižek is engaged in trying to set out the theoretical terms that are necessary for a successful and not merely gestural anti-capitalist project, an attempt that sometimes causes consternation and confusion to those who would prefer something more recognizably practical and who see in Žižek's politics a futile romanticism or a dangerous flirtation with irrationalism.[23]

Traversing the fantasy should not be reduced to some drastic transgressive gesture – anything at such a level could only momentarily disturb the symbolic order – nor can it be modelled along a traditional Marxist line as the drawing back of the curtain of ideological illusions: '"In traversing the fantasy" we do not learn to suspend our phantasmagorical productions' but, instead, see how what happens on the stage is a projection of the audience's participation and, crucially, recognize ourselves occupying the front row seats.[24] An example he gives is that of a rock group who played in Sarajevo when the city was under siege in 1996 during the Bosnian War. In the midst of war and deprivation, the group satirized the city's predicament by utilizing anti-Bosnian clichés to confront the racist stereotypes held by Serbs and others. Instead of trying to deconstruct the bigoted fantasies through a humanist show of 'look, we are like you, we hurt', the fantasy was identified with so as to bring out its core and render it naked.[25]

Žižek is saying that ideology is not a matter of what we think we are doing but what we think we are thinking and this helps explain why he likes to refer to Kafka's parable in *The Trial* about the man from the country seeking admittance at the Door of the Law and waiting there until, grown old and ill, he asks the guard why in all the time he has so patiently waited nobody else has ever come to the Door and sought admittance. The guard answers the dying man and, before shutting the door, tells him it was because the Door was ever only there for him. What this encapsulates for Žižek is how 'the subject failed to include himself in the scene, that is, to take into account how he was not merely an innocent bystander of the spectacle of the Law'.[26] The Law had already taken him into account, addressed him, so that the meaning and excessive reverence that the man from the country attached to the Law – presupposing it as the Other that will confer meaning on the presuppositionless real – only existed because he saw it as transcendent and submitted to seeing himself as excluded from it. What the man does not realize is that his act of seeing himself as an unimportant trifle before the majesty of the Other is what brings about the mystery and transcendent power of the Door of the Law. In Hegelian language, the truth that is finally revealed to the man from the country is that the Absolute was always and already with us or, put another way, Substance and Subject cannot be sundered; the man from the country (Subject) gazed at the Door of the Law (Substance) as something external to himself, not noticing that this distance, the disparity between the two, was at the same time internal to the Door of the Law – its air of mysterious unattainableness was how it perceived its own identity and therefore depended on the man's attitude towards it.[27] In Kant, the substance of what counts as real knowledge, the Thing-in-itself, is indifferent to the knower, the transcendental network of the subject; in Hegel this is not the case because the pathway to knowledge *is* what constitutes knowledge. The worker who comes to see himself as a wage slave is not the same person who previously saw himself as a company employee or a careerist, and the world seen by the proletariat is a different place to what it was before.

Another way of formulating this is to redefine the familiar postmodernism of 'there is no metalanguage' by rejecting the usually concomitant idea that all truth is relative and that whatever is said belongs to a particular discourse and the arbitrary rules governing its particular chain of signifiers. The absence of a metalanguage does not entail this kind of relativism but it does mean there is no neutral position from which to describe the situation. No subject can speak from a neutral position and every subject is already spoken for by the unfathomable split within social reality. The underlying antagonism is not itself writ large, it is the limit that prevents any conception of society as a rational whole, and, instead of reading 'everything is political' as a lame calling card left behind by an outmoded leftism, it can become a statement of the impossibility of ignoring the basic divide, the class struggle, that prevents society being seen as a whole. This is why Žižek criticizes identity politics, post-colonial and queer studies, and politically correct multiculturalism, seeing them as ways of displacing the central antagonism of class conflict and failing to address bigger questions that would politicize the economy. For example, studies of illegal Mexican immigrants in the US by liberal academics tend to imply that economic exploitation is the *result* of racism and intolerance and in this way postmodernism closes down the space for questioning the liberal consensus, for acts that would alter the terms within which it occurs.[28]

The system that defines our existence is a contingent, politically subjective affair, not a necessity spelt by the stars and if our being is recognized as already included in the symbolic order then the possibility always exists for our being to be changed by altering the terms of that order: people who are naïve, 'are not those who think we can break out of our ordinary reality; "naïve" people are those who presuppose this reality as an ontologically self-sufficient given': it is the absence of completeness, the missing links in a putative chain of being, that makes the abyss of freedom a fact and not a fancy.[29] The subject as an autonomous being exists within the space created by the violence of the act. Such an abyss, the underlying absence of any big Other, also rules out notions of necessity in classic Marxist parlance; far from there being any historical, emancipatory fate awaiting the working class or any other class, history is stacked in the opposite direction and the task is to change destiny.

The figure of Antigone, defiantly insisting on a burial for her traitorous brother against the wishes of the king of Thebes, illustrates for Žižek the nature of an act. She grounds her behaviour on the groundlessness of the big Other and it is her *ex nihilo* intervention that stands as an authentic ethical act. It is in

Medea – another female figure from ancient Greek literature who, after learning her husband plans to leave her for a younger woman, kills what are most precious to her husband, their two young children – that Lacan finds a pure example of the fundamental transgression involved in the act. Lacan's other, less horrific example is that of André Gide's wife who, after his death, burned her most precious possession, all his love letters to her. Žižek wishes to insist on what is common to both examples: the sacrifice of what is most precious in order to create the space for a free act that changes the coordinates of what is possible, and he cites other fictional examples such as Sethe's killing of her child in Toni Morrison's *Beloved* and Keyser Soze's decision to shoot his wife and daughter when they are held hostage in *The Usual Suspects*.[30]

Politically though, it is Lenin's ethical act that best represents what is at stake and what is possible.

LENIN'S ACT

The dialectic at work in Kafka's parable about the Door of the Law yields its political significance when it is seen that 'it is his very *inclusion* into the observed scene that allows the subject to achieve *separation* from the big Other'.[31] This goes back to an understanding of the Real not as a barrier, containing the subject within the symbolic and thus at the mercy of the big Other, but as the traumatic antagonism that draws us in and precludes any neutral representation of reality.[32] By way of explaining this, Žižek's account of what happened with Lenin in Russia after February and before October 1917 can be used as an example.[33] The first revolution had taken place, a provisional government established, tsarism deposed and the slate wiped clean – a state of affairs that hurled the Bolsheviks into uncertain and uncharted territory where there was no guarantor, no-one to believe for them. The revolution had not occurred where Marxist orthodoxy thought it inevitable, in Western Europe, and Lenin realized that the catechism preaching obedience to 'objective' laws of historical development could be thrown away. A decisive, 'subjective' and 'untimely' intervention after February would reconfigure the logic that made such an interference premature; Lenin realized there was no big Other of history.

The Mensheviks believed there was a set of historical laws signposting the route to be taken, advising compliance with the democratic revolution and the provisional government while waiting for a revolutionary situation to mature, but Lenin urged otherwise from the moment he arrived at Petrograd's Finland Station on the night of 3 April and delivered a speech denouncing the provisional government that shocked his listeners. He astonished fellow Bolsheviks even more the next day, saying there was unfinished business to be concluded, and was thought reckless if not downright crazy. He became a wanted man by the government and had to go into hiding. The situation revealed subjectivity at its purest, a moment defined by undecidability and the subject confronted with the responsibility of making a choice: 'An Act always involves a radical risk ... it is a step into the open, with no guarantee about the final outcome –why? Because an Act retrospectively changes the very co-ordinates into which it intervenes.'[34]

Lenin experienced the abyss of freedom underpinning Hegel's statement about grasping substance as subject (p. 77). He knew that the contingencies of post-February Russia kept a space open for a new beginning; he was in the eye of a dialectical storm:

> [the Hegelian dialectic] disperses the fetish of 'objective historical process' and allows us to see its genesis: the way the very historical Necessity sprang up as a positivization, as a 'coagulation' of a radically contingent *decision* of the subjects in an open, undecidable situation.[35]

The Bolsheviks, like the other players in the unfolding drama, had to make a decision, a contingent decision that only afterwards could harden into some linear narrative of events. Given the world as ontologically open, constitutively inconsistent, this lack of completeness means that the only sense of necessity or closure that can attach itself to history is inscribed there after the event. Žižek notes how the idea that the past could have been different appeals to right-wing historians but he wants to recognize its place in radical thought, not least because doing so helps to shrug off the burden of historical determinism associated with Marxism.[36] Materialism is not about necessity for there is no objective set of laws that could determine a reality that, ultimately, cannot coincide with itself; and, in an unlikely pairing, Lenin's choice in 1917 is not unlike Kierkegaard's recognition that 'in the last resort there is no theory;

just a fundamental practico-ethical decision about what kind of life one wants to commit oneself to'.[37] There are similarities between Žižek's understanding of the Act and the notion of the Event in the philosophy of Badiou. Both are unforeseeable irruptions of the new that puncture the present, both are an encounter with the Real and carry ethical responsibilities, but Žižek is careful to delineate the nature of an act in such a way that it avoids the risk of being consigned to an unspecificated ontology. He discerns such a risk in Badiou, where an event is 'an abyssal self-grounded autonomous act', as if coming from 'a different ontological dimension'[38] (although the correspondences between Žižek and Badiou in their accounts of how political transformations occur are more telling than the distinctions between them).[39] An act has a miraculous quality but it is not magic and to explain the temporal paradox at work Žižek recalls the sci-fi plot line where someone travels into the past in order to change the present only to subsequently realize that the present he sought to change was brought about *because* of his intervention. What this illustrates is how time seems to follow a linear 'objective' projecture but actually contains within it subjective loops that help account for what happened.[40] The October revolution was eventually, after the event, reinscribed into the 'straight line' of historical time but its happening was unprescribed, dependent on subjective engagements.

What should come after the act is the negation of negation, the challenging task of building a new positive order out of the utopian space that an act makes available. For Žižek, a negative example of this is Mao's failure to follow through the logic of the Cultural Revolution, allowing instead its excesses to remain at the level of carnivalesque destruction, ironically thereby preparing the ground for the equally dizzying dynamic of explosive capitalism that was released under Deng Xiaoping.[41] A symbolic restructuring cannot ignore the unstaunchable *jouissance* that is always capable of derailing what is being put in place, hence the need for an imaginative, revolutionary sublimation that expresses itself not just in the realization of old emancipatory dreams but the inventing of new ways of dreaming and the configuring of new master signifiers. Žižek's trope about new ways of dreaming is more than figurative, for it aligns psychoanalysis with Marxism by insisting that a revolution will not last unless aware of the need to intervene at the level of what is disavowed and replace the libidinal attachments that secured the old order with new ones. By way of an example from cinema, in *The Crying Game* the political programme of the IRA is not rejected *per se* but the film does explore the way in which another kind of personal liberation is also laudable and so for Žižek a suitable subtitle for the movie could have been 'Irishmen, yet another effort, if you want to become republican!'.[42]

FORSAKING THE FATHER

Žižek wants to show how an answer could be found to the question posed by Lenin in his first major piece of writing *What is to be Done?* There is a need for a new beginning motivated not, says Žižek, by what Lacan called the 'narcissism of the lost cause' but in the Beckettian spirit of 'Try again. Fail again. Fail better.'[43] Žižek remarked in an interview how he likes to refer to himself as a Leninist in the spirit of the Lenin of 1915 who, devastated at the betrayal by the left in its support for World War I, admitted the complete failure of the project he had lived for and left for neutral Switzerland where he read Hegel and rethought what had to be done. Similarly today, he goes on, while it is obviously anachronistic to conceive of a revolution by massed ranks of organized labour, it is necessary to rethink the big questions that Lenin asked about how to tackle capitalism and replace it with something better. It is because they asked the right questions that Marx and Lenin should be lauded and not abandoned and the task of trying again is striving towards an ideal. The impulse behind Plato's totalitarian ideal, the French Revolution and October 1917 produced failures but the impulse demands the finding of new expressions because it is part of our species-being: 'communism is for me a platonic idea'.[44]

It is in this context that one should position the interest that Žižek the avowed atheist brings to Christianity. Belief is an act that arises from a decision and Žižek, beginning with his first book in English, likes to refer for this reason to Pascal's advice that doubting subjects should act as if they believe and they will come to really believe.[45] Belief is not guaranteed by knowledge, just as in Hegel there is no spirit of a super-Subject guiding history: 'Therein resides the paradox of [Hegel's] "objective spirit": it is independent of individuals, encountered by them as given, preexisting them, as the presupposition of their activity, yet it is nonetheless spirit, that is, something that exists only in so far as individuals relate their activity to it, only as *their* (pre)supposition'.[46] Pascal and Hegel are seen to share an understanding of how belief as action, decision manifested, comes before belief as an inward state of mind (which, by the way, helps explain why Wittgenstein's favourite type of film was the Western, a genre whose aesthetic is grounded on just such an insight). The paradox resides in the way a ritual, like that of getting down on one's knees to pray, retroactively produces the idea that the ritual was observed because of one's belief when really it is the other way around.

St Paul's call for a community of believers, struggling to create a new order of existence, is akin to Žižek's belief that effective political change will only come about when accompanied by a commitment to the creation of a new structure of subjectivity. Žižek's objection to celebrations of the plasticity of identity and how we should all construct our own versions of who we are is that such paeans to post-modernity do not contest but complement the fluid dynamics of contemporary capitalism. Notions of identity that speak of plurality and the nomadic reflect the world we live in but changing this world involves a different kind of language, the kind found in St Paul's Epistle to the Romans (7.7) stating how sin cannot be divorced from law because prohibition engenders desire for what is prohibited. This shares a kinship with the logic of Hegel's dialectic and it entails, for St Paul, asking if we should not carry on sinning for the sake of increasing grace (6.1): God being our saviour only if we indulge in sin. Žižek spells out how St Paul's insight and his alarm at its implications leads to a subject divided between willingly obeying the law while unconsciously desiring to break with it. The conscious obedient self has in a sense 'died' because it is the impulse to sin that affirms itself and when St Paul asks 'how shall we who died to sin live in it' (6.2) Žižek reformulates his question: 'How would it be possible for me to experience my life-impulse not as a foreign automatism, as a blind "compulsion to repeat", making me transgress the law, with the unacknowledged complicity of the law itself, but as a fully subjectivized, positive "Yes!" to my life?'[47] Žižek warms to St Paul's call for deliverance from the superego, the 'way of the flesh' generated by the law (7.5), through a suspension of the big Other that allows for everything but which, mediated by the love that is the 'way of the spirit', disciplines choice: 'All things are lawful for me, but not all things beneficial. All things are lawful for me, but I will not be dominated by anything' (1 Cor. 6:12). What is valued here, amongst other things, is the stress on responsibility, risk-taking and the making of a decision – the qualities that endear Žižek to Westerns like Delmer Daves' *3:10 to Yuma* and *The Hanging Tree* and Zack Snyder's *300*[48] – and the unconditional love that St Paul speaks of can translate into the idea of communism.[49]

Why does Žižek not develop what has just been outlined as a humanist project, without a recourse to the importance of Christianity? The reason is that he sees humanism as contained within limits that exclude changing what seems unchangeable; notions that speak of realizing one's potential, discovering the true Self, do not allow for a return to the very beginning and a reinvention of the Self – 'in short, *to change Eternity itself* (*what we "always-already are"*)'[50] – whereas theology is a name for just such a dimension, one that engages with fundamental issues about subjectivity, belief and the necessary conditions for a transformation of the socio-economic system. These fundamental issues lead to the bedrock upon which our universe of meaning is built, the presuppositions that have always already been made and the orientation already taken, the primordial fantasy that shapes the contours by which we live, and Christianity's act of faith is the belief that the fantasy can be traversed, the orientation transformed: 'the Christian 'Good News (Gospel)' is that it is possible to suspend the burden of the past, to cut the ropes which tie us to our past deeds, to wipe the slate and begin again from zero ... a New Beginning is possible.'[51] Christian theology, in kinship with Schelling's theosophy, creates the ontological space that the Act requires and the basis for a materialist account of change. Talk of God creating the world *ex nihilo* is not mystical nonsense since 'God *is already there*' and designates the paradox of 'Something (a meaningful order) "miraculously" emerging out of nothing from the preceding chaos'.[52]

Žižek's post-secularist 'theological turn' is pointedly political and resoundingly atheist and while he avoids the kind of nebulous uncertainty about the actual existence of God that mars Eagleton's defence of theology, he shares with Eagleton the conviction that the religious sensibility can address what is too often occluded from secular discourses.[53] Christianity for Žižek confronts the non-existence of the onto-theological big Other when Christ is abandoned on the cross and asks 'Father, why did you forsake me?', a moment that reveals the impotence of God-the-Father and makes Christ truly human, transmuting the gap between God and man into a breach within God himself:

> The only way for God to create free people (humans) is to open up the space for them in HIS OWN lack/void/gap: man's existence is the living proof of God's self-limitation ... Love is always love for the Other insofar as he is lacking – we love the Other BECAUSE of his limitation, helplessness, ordinariness even.[54]

Pagan notions of the divine, content to rejoice in a sense of an attainable spiritual perfection, cannot reach this materialist realm which, instead of figuring a journey towards the truth, embraces the uncomfortable idea of an encounter that breaks with the pretence of balance and harmony.[55] This is something the Catholic writer G. K. Chesterton endorses and celebrates when he explains his theological convictions and it has a lot to do with Žižek's fondness for this writer.[56] Žižek's jokes are legion but one worth retelling in this context concerns three Russian political prisoners in a cell, one of whom explains how he has been sentenced to five years for opposing Popov (a real victim of Stalin's purges) while the second, prey to a change in the party line, is serving ten years for supporting him and the third trumps them by announcing he has been jailed for life and he *is* Popov; this is transposed onto a theological plane with 'I was thrown to the lions in the arena for believing in Christ!' 'I was burned at the stake for ridiculing Christ' 'I died on a cross, and I *am* Christ!'[57] When we share the moment on the cross and realize there is no paternal, transcendent Other, divine or otherwise, to provide answers, then Christianity becomes 'the religion of atheism'.[58]

For Žižek, Christ's moment on the cross bespeaks a universe lacking the wholeness that could bind being into a totality, a cosmic dissonance and impotence, an encounter with the Real that throws everything out of joint. The obscene superego has always kept secret the impotence of the big Other but Christ reveals this secret (there is no bigger big Other than God) and Christianity jettisons the split between the official symbolic order and its unofficial obscene supplement:

> For a Christian believer, the fact that he does not do certain things is based not on prohibitions (which then generate the transgressive desire to indulge precisely in these things) but in the

positive, affirmative attitude of love, which renders meaningless the accomplishment of acts that bear witness to the fact that I am not free but still dominated by an external force.[59]

This tumbling of the symbolic order brings ethics into play, presenting the subject with a choice: to disavow the moment and retreat or to accept the encounter and reboot, reorganizing the fantasmatic coordinates of the symbolic universe that structure identity. This presents ethical challenges – some of which are explored in Atom Egoyan's film *The Sweet Hereafter* and Lasse Hallsrtöm's *The Cider House Rules*[60] – but figures as different as St Paul and Lenin rose to the challenge because they discerned the parallax gap that makes a new beginning possible. They also bear testimony to the need for an ethical commitment to eternal ideas of universality, of the kind preached by St Paul and made available by the death of Christ and the coming of the Holy Ghost, a community of believers functioning without the need for a big Other. Žižek employs the language of Christianity because secular humanism cannot give force to the theological form of thought that allows us to say that 'it is not we who are acting, but a higher force that is acting through us'.[61] This is not the big Other but a sense of collective purpose that would be part of a new structure of subjectivity; and the legacy of Christ's death on the cross is God as the final ethical agency who leaves us with the burden and duty of organizing our existence and retaining fidelity to a Cause. Communism is both this Cause and the fidelity necessary to create and sustain it. The idea that Christ's death as a human brings about a sublation and the rebirth of the Holy Spirit is reinscribed by Žižek who sees instead the Spirit as 'a *virtual* entity', a 'subjective presupposition' that, like Communism, actualizes itself when subjects assume its existence and act accordingly. This in essence is Žižek's Hegelian theology –

What is sublated in the move from the Son to Holy Spirit is thus God himself: after the Crucifixion, the death of God incarnate, the universal God returns as a Spirit of the community of believers, i.e., he is the one who passes from being a transcendent substantial Reality to a virtual/ideal entity which exists only as the 'presupposition' of acting individuals. The standard perception of Hegel as an organicist holist who thinks that really existing individuals are just 'predicates' of some 'higher' substantial

Whole, epiphenomena of the Spirit as a mega-Subject who effectively runs the show, totally misses this crucial point.[62]

– and the conclusion it leads to is that 'only atheists can truly believe' because only atheists can abandon the big Other of a higher Reality and yet still believe in a Cause; similarly, in a way that Žižek emphasizes by quoting the anarchist Durruti – 'The only church that illuminates is a burning church' – and transposing its anti-clericalism to signify how only Christianity makes available a space deep enough to bury the big Other, 'a true religion arrives at its truth only through its self-cancellation'. [63]

The point that such a Hegelian understanding will inevitably be diluted if it is confined to the vocabulary of humanism is worth dwelling on because it helps in an understanding of why Žižek likes to draw attention to the 'inhuman' dimension. It is only through a recognition of the inhuman in the makeup of humanity – the Holocaust being a witness to this truth – that an ethics after Auschwitz can make a claim on our fidelity; and this comes about through a negation of the negation that by diminishing the individual life allows for the universal to make its claim; and the viability of such a claim is championed by Žižek when he quotes as a conclusion to this line of argument words from Robespierre's last speech before he was arrested and executed:

> But there do exist, I can assure you, souls that are feeling and pure: it exists, that tender, imperious and irresistible passion, the torment and delight of magnanimous hearts; that deep horror of tyranny, that compassionate zeal for the oppressed, that sacred love for the homeland, that even more holy love for humanity, without which a great revolution is just a noisy crime that destroys another crime; it does exist, that generous ambition to establish here on earth the world's first Republic.[64]

DICTATORSHIP OF THE PROLETARIAT

The theological frame of reference translates 'on the ground' into an unashamed and deliberately provocative evocation of the need for a dictatorship of the proletariat and Žižek brings a hard-nosed edge of realism to what might be seen as utopianism in St Paul's call for a new beginning. Christianity provides for Žižek a way of establishing what is necessary for the kind of political change that is felt to be necessary, just as communism provides a term for the kind of society that could be ushered in by a radical politics. Dictatorship of the proletariat – 'the only true choice today[65] – is a radical democracy based on a universal principle of egalitarianism and, recognizing that state power is always a form of dictatorship, it is a state order that would replace the liberal democracy that represents the dictatorship of capitalism. Liberal democracy, a 'biopolitical administration of life' based on fear and exercised through procedures that regulate the choosing of who will exert this power[66], excludes those who are relegated to a subordinate place within the social edifice and it this class that Žižek reclaims as the proletariat. Those who are 'the part of those who have no part'[67] represent what is universal and Žižek has no illusions about what is involved in building a social edifice based upon such a universalism. He tackles the brutal fact that violence is an inescapable part of the world we live in, one of his books is devoted to the topic, but there are important differences between various types of violence and when it comes to the violent act of radically changing how we live Žižek emphasizes the crucial need to prepare the ground beforehand. In what could be taken as a gloss on the guiding principle underlying his own political project, Žižek states the issue at stake:

> and there is the violent act of actually changing the basic coordinates of a constellation. In order for the last kind of violence to take place, *the very place should be opened up* through a gesture of pure withdrawal in which – to quote *Mallarmé* – *rien n'aura eu lieu que le lieu*, nothing will have taken place but the place itself.[68]

Žižek gives a positive spin to the use of the idea of violence in a way that is similar to his affirmative and provocative employment of the term terror, reappropriating them from their monopolization by the right-wing and reinventing them for an emancipatory project that is as ethical as it is political. The 'place' that he is referring to is correlate with the impact of fully assuming the non-existence of the big Other: 'even if we concede that we cannot ever occupy its place … there must be a standard which allows us to take the measure of our acts and pronounce their "true meaning", their true ethical status'.[69] This, he goes on to explain, is precisely what Lenin achieved when he overrode objections to a second revolution and assumed a revolutionary act outside of the big Other. The violence that may be the result of occupying such a place is not the same as the other meaning of the word – 'great force, severity, or vehemence, intensity of some condition or influence' (*Oxford English Dictionary*) – and Žižek is far from giving a carte blanche to acts of violence even though he unflinchingly accepts that revolutionary events, like the French Revolution, may entail physical violence. Such violence is 'divine' and can only be disavowed if, quoting Robespierre's retort to the moderates, what is wanted is 'a revolution without a revolution'.[70] An instance of the nuanced approach that is brought to the topos of violence and revolution is evident in Žižek's comment on the 2005 film *V for Vendetta*. Given that V, the political dissident, sets out to succeed where Guy Fawkes failed and thereby bring down Suter's totalitarian rule of Britain, one might be inclined to think this could be endorsed as a fictional example of 'divine violence' but Žižek is not convinced and detects instead similarities and parallels between V's furious vendetta and Suter's institutional violence; it fails to draw out the kind of Hegelian 'identity of opposites' found in Chesterton's novel *The Man Who Was Thursday* (where the anarchist leader and the police chief are one and the same) or Shelley's 'The Mask of Anarchy'.[71] A film that is praised for envisioning an unproblematic sense of meaningful resistance, Alfonso Cuáron's *Children of Men*, does not side with The Fishes, the underground group employing violence against the right-wing government, but with the metaphoric force of the final image of the hero floating alone out at sea in a rowboat. In his commentary included in the film's DVD release Žižek identifies as 'the condition of the renewal' the need to 'cut your roots', a restatement of Lacan's saying *Le grand Autre n'existe pas* (the big Other does not exist).[72] This translates as the need to forego all invariables and in a specific context of violence and revolution this would include any simplistic notion that the overthrow of a government by physical violence necessarily leads to an improved state of affairs.

The expressed admiration for *Children of Men* comes from its cinematic quality, its filmic rendering of political concerns that turns the global infertility affecting all women, the narrative drive of the film, into 'the true infertility [which] is the lack of meaningful historical experience' and which emerges as the background to the events being played out. Žižek's respect for the film is not indicative of his messianic hope in a better world yet to come, a hopelessly impractical and visionary gesture on his part, and it should be put alongside his recognition of the need for a political party that would set about implementing a communist revolution – 'the key "Leninist" lesson today is: politics without the organizational form of the Party is politics without politics'[73] – because an emancipatory politics cannot be achieved from the sidelines. The state as the locus of power has to be engaged with, not withdrawn from anarchistically in the hope that alternative spaces of political autonomy will eventually coalesce into a new form of living. When a book appeared that argued for just such a strategy, Simon Critchley's *Infinitely Demanding*, Žižek disparaged it for the same kind of reasons he gave in *The Parallax View* (2006c) –

> all is needed is a slight shift in our perspective, and all the activity of 'resistance', of bombarding those in power with impossible "subversive" (ecological, feminist, antiracist, antiglobalist ...) demands, looks like an internal process of feeding the machine of power, providing the material to keep it in motion.[74]

– citing the 2003 anti-war marches against the invasion of Iraq as an example of what becomes a symbiosis between the powerless and those in power. The protestors embodied the 'beautiful soul' syndrome in Hegel, the safe enjoyment of yearning for an idea and descrying the sad state of a debased world that puts the ideal out of reach, while the war leaders could not only, equally safely, ignore the demonstrations as a possible threat to their policy but profit from them by using such behaviour as an example of the democratic spirit they were protecting by invading tyrannous Iraq.[75]

A contemporary real-world example for Žižek of what needs to be done is to be found instead in Hugo Chávez's Venezuela, a country where the party is trying to build a new form of politics outside of parliament, while past attempts like those of the French Revolution or China's Cultural Revolution can be applauded even though they occasioned much terrible violence and ended in failure. Žižek is not glorifying extreme violence when he looks with approval to figures like Robespierre but drawing attention to the fatal weakness of orthodox left-wing praxis that is mired in liberal democracy. There is a force choice being offered between liberal democracy or Stalinist-type dictatorship when what is needed is a shift of the ground, a redefinition of what is possible and what class war now means, and this is only possible when the 'zero-level antagonism' between the excluded and the included is recognized.[76] What Žižek's examples have in common and they range from the Jacobins' homes for the elderly, to Bolshevik attempts to find alternatives for the ritual of funerals to Chávez's militarizing of barrios – is a politicization of state power that extends into the public space in ways not deemed legitimate in liberal democracy, a political and a cultural revolution:

> [factual revolution plus spiritual reform, namely, actual struggle for the transformation of customs, of the substance of everyday life – what Hegel called the 'silent weaving of the Spirit', which undermines the invisible foundations of power.[77]

Žižek has a withering contempt for those who find comfort in *bien-pensant* pieties and he looks instead to the figure of Bartleby in Melville's novella *Bartleby, the Scrivener: A Story of Wall Street* who repeatedly turns down invitations with the polite refusal 'I would prefer not to'. Part of what needs to be declined is the kind of busying activity that only ostensibly is concerned with change – 'in which we are active all the time to make sure that nothing will really change' – when the essential first step is to withdraw and decline opportunities to participate in what ultimately only serves to strengthen the system by co-opting us into it.[78] Bartleby's passivity is to be understood as an aggressive political stance, as when Leonidas at Thermopylae declines Xerxes' one simple request to kneel in acknowledgement of Persian power,[79] a refusal to conform that is the necessary act of withdrawal without which the violence that is necessarily a part of revolutionary change will become just another 'noisy crime'.

There is something enigmatic about the use of the Bartleby figure but in the light of what Žižek says about the need for a Party and a dictatorship of the proletariat it is a misunderstanding to think that he is indulging in gestural politics or conceiving of political change in individualist terms.[80] As Jodi Dean has discerned, Bartleby can be read as a progressive example of what is implicit in the nature of a political myth as defined by Žižek when he is looking at the *Star Wars* saga: 'a political myth proper is not so much a narrative with some determinate political meaning but, rather, an empty container of a multitude of inconsistent, even mutually exclusive, meanings ...'[81]

The idea of a political myth as a set of potentially contra-dictory meanings is related to Žižek's notion of difference through repetition, the motif referred to at the start of this chapter in relation to Benjamin's *Theses on the Philosophy of History* and the paradoxical sense of the past being unpredictable. It is seen to relate to the notion of becoming in Deleuze:

> Becoming is thus strictly correlative to the concept of REPETITION: far from being opposed to the emergence of the New, the proper Deleuzian paradox is that something truly New can *only* emerge through repetition. What repetition repeats is not the way the past 'effectively was' but the *virtuality* inherent to the past and betrayed by its past actualization. In this precise sense, the emergence of the New changes the past itself, that is, it retrospectively changes not the actual past – we are not in science fiction – but the balance between actuality and virtuality in the past.[82]

Žižek is drawn to the potency of this idea and returns to it in his more recent writings.[83] It becomes his way of reading Heidegger's triadic, circular structure for the temporality of *Dasein*, its movement from the future through the past to the present: in its projects for the future being is coming-back-to-itself but always within-the-world, absorbed and constituted by a historicity, a having-been-ness. The cognitive inflection that Žižek brings to this Heideggerian analysis is to situate the future in the past not, of course, through a closed loop of time that endlessly circles back on itself but in the vertiginous and emancipatory sense that anything that might come to pass was there as a possibility in the past but not realized at the time.[84] This is how Lenin is to be repeated, retrieving not just the impulse that he acted upon after February 1917 when he saw the possibility of a second revolution but repossessing the opportunity that he failed to bring to fruition. This emphatically and necessarily does not imply a return to a highly centralized party and all that is pejorative in the term 'Leninist' but, in today's times, when capitalism is being naturalized and communism risks becoming some chiliastic utopia, the resolve and intent to change the order of power and not be channelled into forms of resistance that only strengthens the status quo is more imperative than ever.[85] It is why, when we are living in the end times, lost causes are worth defending; Žižek's project, lasting a lot longer than Lacan's short sessions but inspired by them, is to bring this home so that we can get off the couch, armed with the violent, positive power of negativity, and begin, as Ghandi put it, to be the change that we want to see in the world – but with a minimal though sublime difference, a shift of perspective that marks a passage from resignation to rapture, allowing us to enact not a quietist pacifism of the spirit but, instead, passive aggression.

CHAPTER FIVE

READING ŽIŽEK

The date for each book below refers to the year of first publication, not to the year of the particular edition listed in the references.

THE SUBLIME OBJECT OF IDEOLOGY (1989)

His first book to be published in English, *The Sublime Object of Ideology* came out in 1989 and for new readers of Žižek it is a good place to begin acclimatizing oneself to the author's voice and style of writing. The prose is lucid and there is a clarity to the thought, even when it not always clear where an explication is going or, indeed, where it has come from. The book's gathering pace of thought and compacted layers of ideas still make a heady read, but without some acquaintance with Lacan and Hegel it is easy to lose the thread and feel overwhelmed. While Marxism is kept at a distance in *The Sublime Object of Ideology*, it is used as an illustration of the 'quilting point' (*point de caption*) and seen as limited by a too-hasty historicism, the space for a rapprochement may be detected in the close attention paid to Benjamin's *Theses on the Philosophy of History* (pp. 136–42).

The opening pages are devoted to Freud and the three different levels of a dream: the surface 'text', the latent thought and the unconscious desire. What is important about a dream is its form, the way in which one of these levels, desire, interposes itself between the other two levels. Similarly, it is argued, what is important for Marx about the commodity is its form, exemplified in the way the commodity money becomes a sublime material with a fetishistic quality. The unconscious is at work in both cases: dreams and commodities involve a level of knowledge that is not available to the participants. In the social field this knowledge is the ideological;

its symptom being an immanent moment of imbalance, 'a species subverting its own genus',[1] as when the commodity labour produces a surplus value that is then appropriated by one party in the exchange of labour for payment. At some point, the reader begins to wonder where this is all leading, but like a film or novel that begins with seemingly unconnected episodes it is a matter of staying with it and waiting to see how the scenes will join up. Umberto Eco's *The Name of the Rose* is introduced to criticize the notion that for Žižek has too hastily become a hallmark of contemporary thinkers, the idea of a post-ideological world where signs and signifiers just giddily circulate with no underlying message. Seeing the world in this way does not disturb what is identified as the ideological fantasy: the masking of society's division and the suturing of this traumatic kernel by means of providing the subject with an identity outside the big Other. This is what the overture – the opening sections of the first chapter – has been announcing: in dreams and in ideology we approach the Real of our desire but the kind of cynical reason that characterizes Eco's novel points to that part of us that does not want to awaken and confront the traumatic imbalance at the heart of matters. This imbalance is the contradiction that drives capitalism, it is the excess of surplus enjoyment and surplus value.

In the rest of Part I and in Part II many ideas are introduced that Žižek will develop, repeat and expand in the years to come: changing the narration of the past through psychoanalysis and, in the public sphere, by subjective engagement; the nature of the Hegelian dialect (as traced in Jane Austin's book *Pride and Prejudice*); the nature of the Real; the subversive position of the hysteric, and the *Che vuoi?* (what do you want?) of the Other. This question emerges in the course of Žižek's explication of Lacan's four graphs of desire. The first graph maps the 'quilting' of the 'pre-symbolic' individual into the chain of signification, an interpellation achieved by the address of a master signifier which effaces its own traces by a retroactive process, producing the divided subject. The second graph shows the 'voice' as the remainder of the signifier after the quilting process. The subject now identifies with a trait of the big Other, taking upon himself a name or mandate, and this is distinct from the assumption of an imaginary self-identification which gives the illusion of autonomous agency. The latter is how we would like to see ourselves while in symbolic identity we identify with the gaze from which we are observed, but the two identities cannot simply be opposed. A limitation in Dickens is discerned because although there is an imaginary identification with the dispossessed it emanates from a gaze of the well-off and powerful within the symbolic order. Another example, Woody Allen's *Play It Again, Sam*, is used to show how symbolic identity dissolves the imaginary after the subject assumes his place in the symbolic network. The third graph focuses on the opening that is left after the quilting process has symbolically and arbitrarily fixed meaning, a gap out of which the subject is driven to ask why he is positioned where he is in the symbolic order (Cary Grant's predicament in *North by Northwest*). The unfathomable aspect to the desire of the Other, its triggering of the enigma of one's own desire and the role of fantasy is cogently summarized in the 'Fantasy as a Screen for the Desire of the Other' section (pp. 118–21). The fourth graph adds *jouissance* and shows *castration* occurring when the body is filtered through the signifier, thus bringing to the fore the discordance between the big Other and enjoyment. What is left are 'erogenous zones', places of enjoyment around which Freudian drive circulates and which Žižek hazards equating with the Lacanian formula of *sinthome*. The remainder, surplus-enjoyment, is manipulated by ideology and structured in fantasy as a support that masks the hollow core; and here Žižek introduces the figure of the Jew, an example he will return to many times in his later books.

The final section, Part III, begins with more Lacanian notions and settles into a sustained elucidation of the real (pp. 161–4, 169–73) and the nature of the subject before Hegelian thought gradually makes its presence felt. Up until now the book has been mostly concerned with Lacanian motifs and the reader has always been able to temporarily turn aside and look to secondary literature for help with an understanding of key psychoanalytic terms. A difficulty arises when a reader tries to do the same for Hegel only to find his or her puzzlement compounded by the fact that Žižek's understanding of Hegel does not fit the approach of most standard interpretations. It is better to use one's grasp of what has been said about Lacan as a way into Hegel, as indeed does Žižek when he concludes his exposition of the 'negation of the negation' by drawing in the subject's *Che vuoi?* and the enigma it creates (pp. 176–8). Just as the puzzled subject has to realize that the Other is equally beset by the urgency of a question that encapsulates the lack at the heart of symbolic communication, so too does the 'negation of the negation' lead to the realization that the experience of negation is a positive condition of identity. The correspondences that Žižek finds between aspects of Lacanian and Hegelian thought lead to the book's final chapter which leaves Lacan in the background and focuses instead on the pivotal philosophical difference between Hegel and Kant regarding the Thing-in-itself. The Kantian Sublime (pp. 202–4) retains the Thing-in-itself in a negative mode, a fissure that results from a necessary but noble failure to adequately represent what is unrepresentable, but in Hegel the negativity goes all the way down and the Thing-in-itself *is* this negativity, the void that is the self-relating inadequacy of appearance to be anything other than itself. The Sublime embodies the nothingness that is beyond the realm of the phenomenal. The final sections (pp. 207–31) are the densest pages in *The Sublime Object of Ideology*, rapidly covering Hegelian ground to reiterate the association between the Lacanian Thing, the *objet a* of fantasy that fills the void, and Hegel's statement from his dialectic of phrenology that 'the *being of Spirit is a bone*'.[2] The bone also fills out the void that is the failure of signification and this leads Žižek into deeper Hegelian territory: the dialectic, the positing of presuppositions, reflection and substance as subject. At some point in these final pages, many readers realize to their dismay that Žižek is taking for granted the reader's thorough acquaintance with *The Phenomenology of Spirit* and *The Logic of Science*.

FOR THEY KNOW NOT WHAT THEY DO (1991)

Towards the end of *The Sublime Object of Ideology* the book's centre of gravity began to shift from Lacan to Hegel and in Žižek's next book, published two years later, this change in orientation becomes firmer. Aspects of Hegelian thought are the main focus, linking up with psychoanalytic concerns whenever possible, and the 2002 edition of *For They Know Not What They Do* includes a lengthy forward in which the author ranks it as a more substantial book than his previous one, characterizing it as a work of theory rather than a 'succession of anecdotes and cinema references'. A theoretical work it certainly is and the reader is quickly immersed in the deep end of Hegelian thought as Žižek explores dialectical movement, coming at it from different directions and applying it to a range of situations. 'Negation of the negation', pictured as a doubling movement of mirroring and inversion, can be described from a variety of perspectives and this multi-directional approach is what characterizes the book.

For They Know Not What They Do is not at first the easiest of books to get into, partly due to the style of writing and partly because of the subject matter. The style is initially rather dry and explications seem convoluted, with jokes and references to pop-culture noticeable by their absence, and it takes a while for the reader to adjust and settle down into a series of refined observations on Hegelian topics like identity, the universal and particular, substance and subject and theories of judgement. What was said earlier about the final parts of *The Sublime Object of Ideology* applies more insistently to this book: some acquaintance with *The Phenomenology of Spirit* and *The Logic of Science* is necessary and, given that *The Logic of Science* is hardly a familiar text even for most philosophy students or scholars, many readers will find themselves grappling not so much with Žižek's treatment of Hegel as with the Hegelian ideas themselves. For instance, as part of the endeavour to explain how there is no teleology of Reason in history and how 'absolute knowledge' can be modelled as a state of coming to recognize how the searcher produces what was being searched for (pp. 167–71) Žižek turns to Hegel's account of reflection in *The Logic of Science*. But this account of reflection is intrinsically difficult and poses it own challenge of interpretation, although Žižek tries to help (endnote 37 on p. 174) by using the example of different approaches to the reading of a text, a case in point that came up first in *The Sublime Object of Ideology*.[3]

For They Know Not What They Do begins on Lacanian ground, in the semiotic field where the Master Signifier S1 operates as the One, quilting a field of non-totalized signifiers into a consistent whole. By its unique position, the One represents a moment of impossibility: it does not represent what the field of other signifiers have failed to represent – it cannot do so for, like the barred subject, $, there is no signifier that can represent this void – but what it does do is reflect the failure into itself and this movement of reversal leads into Hegelian territory. An example of this kind of reversal in the book's first chapter, apropos of the anti-Semitic forces in the Dreyfus affair, is the newspaper letter that turned an apparent failure, the suicide of an intelligence officer clearly pointing to the innocence of Dreyfus, into an indication of the man's guilt and a vindication of the right-wing's position. Other examples follow – bringing in St Paul,

Mozart, Racine, films from Hitchcock and Francis Ford Coppola – to show a movement of reversal, with something turning out to be very different from what is expected, but not a simple inversion. Hegel's sublation, and this is the point of the exercise, is not about two coming to be one but about a 'remarking', a doubling that comes about through a change of perspective. Žižek understands the notion of a rational totality and absolute knowledge in Hegel as a recognition of how one totalization 'begets' another (p. 99) and the 'class struggle is *real* in the Lacanian sense' because it occasions attempted totalizations: 'an impediment which gives rise to ever-new symbolizations by means of which one endeavours to integrate and domesticate it' (p.100).

The nature of identity in Hegel is also described in a way that sees it not as an indicator of something unchanging but its opposite ('We come across identity when predicates fail'), as including the empty place it occupies. The law, for example, equals crime in the way that transgression is what gives rise to it. Identity-with-itself, as in 'the law is the law', 'God is God', occurs when an entity encounters its own void, its lack of positivity and absence of predicates. A constant theme running through *For They Know Not What They Do* is that Hegel is not to be read in terms of a closed system ruled by a teleological imperative nor from a Derridean orthodoxy which allows for an excess, a supplement, left over after the moment of sublation. Žižek stresses self-division, the obstacle that is inherent, the negativity at the core of every positive identity. Chapter Four ties some of these points together with the notion of Hegelian dialectics as 'hysterical', a dramatizing that makes manifest the unspoken presuppositions sustaining the consistency of a subject's position. An example from Hegel's own work is found in the analysis of the ascetic's position in the Unhappy Consciousness section of *The Phenomenology of Spirit*: the ascetic, like the hysteric, converts the impediment into a desire for impediment so that desire is maintained. Another example of this logic is found in Kant's sublime where the impediment, in this case the impossibility of encountering the Thing-in-itself, is converted into the experience of the sublime. The negative is not absorbed in a moment of self-mediation on the path to a fuller totality; instead, the negative is the making positive of, the materialization of, negativity.

Žižek finds the dialectical process at work in the philosophy of the later Wittgenstein (pp. 145–56) because of the way he tackles a philosophical problem not by trying to peer into its putative essence but by withdrawing from it 'in-itself' and looking instead at how the key term is used, staging the presuppositions at work in the context and circumstances of the term's employment. This reformulation of the 'problem' effects a displacement, a change of perspective, that brings the hidden presuppositions to the surface.

Chapter Four addresses fantasy and the nature of the gaze, the impossible act of witnessing one's own genesis, explaining it as a way of dealing with the closed synchrony of the symbolic order and the circular causality of language in always referring only to itself. The impossible gaze is a way of connecting this order with a point of origin, creating a 'missing link' in a chain that would otherwise be seamless. The book's final chapter starts with Kantian ethics but hops around the existing political situation – remember this is 1991 and the seemingly global triumph of liberal democracy – before concluding with a Lacanian rally to look trauma in the face and keep faith with the point of impossibility, the drive that drives the ethical.

LOOKING AWRY (1991)

In order for an otherwise ordinary object to be seen as possessing the sublimity that makes it an *objet petit a* it cannot simply be looked at directly because then we only see the object for what it is. The anti-Semite does not look at a Jew in the street and just see a person belonging to a particular ethnic group, he views a representative of those who behind the scenes manipulate and control the social order; the anti-Semite sees his stand-in for the class antagonisms that cry out for an explanation, one capable of bearing the brunt of his dissatisfaction. The anti-Semite has to look at the Jew obliquely, sublimation requires anamorphosis, and the title of this book provides the metaphor for its theoretical thrust (with the help of some lines from *Richard II* where Shakespeare himself finds it difficult to verbally straighten out the metaphor).

For the unwary reader, the subtitle of *Looking Awry – An Introduction to Jacques Lacan Through Popular Culture* – might suggest a relatively easy way to begin learning more about Lacan and Žižek, and there is a wealth of potted summaries of the short stories and films that aid in the understanding of what is being said about them. At the same time, though, the book requires a nodding acquaintance with terms such as *objet petit a*, the symbolic order, the

Real, the big Other and so on. The superego, in particular, is a key term in the analysis of Hitchcock (it helps to have watched films such as *Vertigo*, *Psycho* and *The Birds*) and interpretation of Kafka, and equally important is the idea of the gaze as formulated for the first time in *Looking Awry*: 'When I look at an object, the object is always already gazing at me, and from a point at which I cannot see it.'[4] The cinematic use of the gaze, rendering it as being on the side of the object, marking the point when the viewed object returns the gaze (as in *Rear Window*'s pivotal moment when the murderer looks back at James Stewart or towards the end of *Psycho* when Lilah climbs the hill to the house of Norman and his 'mother' and it is the house that gazes back at her (pp. 117–18), is important to Žižek and he returns to it in *The Fright of Real Tears*.[5] In Looking Awry he also uses the idea of the gaze in an interesting way to account for the way we are fascinated by the gaze of the mythical 1940s audience of film noir who believe for us in the films and how the logic of such nostalgia reflects on itself in *Shane*, *Body Heat* and *Driver*. In *Rear Window* Žižek reads the gaze as the means for the James Stewart character to deal with his sexual angst by projecting onto the scenes of the apartments opposite his window his worries about what married life with the Grace Kelly character might turn out to be. In his later work, Žižek is interested in the philosophical significance that can be read into the uncanny functioning of the gaze as the Hegelian inversion of subject and object.[6]

A motif of the 'maternal superego' is traced in Hitchcock (p. 99) and *Looking Awry* draws to an end by returning to the superego but with reflections of a political rather a cinematic kind. The superego as the obscene law that feeds off our enjoyment becomes the 'stain' that ruins the cosy colouring of a liberal utopia where public law protects private fantasies. In broader terms, the utopian element in democracy should be acknowledged as the abstract, formal nature of the individuals that are envisaged as making up its substance. Such a recognition is missing, as is the realization that democracy depends on the capacity of the nation-state to materialize enjoyment in the form of nationalist myths and xenophobic exclusions of those seen not to share in the same way the 'national Thing'. Patriotism becomes the last refuge for enjoyment.

ENJOY YOUR SYMPTOM! (1992)

The subtitle, *Jacques Lacan in Hollywood and Out*, indicates the range of subject matter and the fact that the approach throughout is firmly Lacanian. The latest edition, published in 2008, includes a new preface by the author.

The first chapter explores aspects of intersubjectivity, beginning with Chaplin's films and focusing on how the final scene in *City Lights* captures the fraught moment of exposure when – the flower girl recognizing the tramp as the reality of her fantasy benefactor – a subject is seen without the support of the gentrifying representations of the symbolic network. This moment is viewed as an example of when 'the letter arrives at its destination', a phrase Lacan used and which Žižek artfully employs in the rest of the chapter to explore issues of an existential nature.

The films of Rossellini, principally *Germany Year Zero, Europa '51* and *Stromboli*, are used in the second chapter to illustrate another traumatic moment: an alienated individual, contracted out from the symbolic order, confronts the nullity that underlies it and steps into the abyss of the Real. In part two of this chapter (pp. 53–63) there is a lucid summary of the Lacanian and Hegelian background against which this psychotic contracting out and divorcing from the big Other is positioned.

Chapter Three has a virtuoso quality as Žižek spins a set of dialectically driven examples around ideas of choice, repetition, master signifiers and the act. It begins with the 'forced choice' (an example given by Lacan is that of the highwayman's 'your money or your life' call – choose life and you lose your money anyway – where the choice is made for you) that underlies our entry into the symbolic order. Terms like incest taboo and symbolic castration, employed to characterize the nature of our entry into community life, do not refer to a negotiated settlement – as if the person being robbed could offer just a percentage of his money in return for his life – for we do not freely choose to enter the symbolic order; socialization entails that the choice has already been made. What though if this original 'choice', the one constituting our social identity, can be repeated but in a way that produces a different decision? Such a repetition may be suicidal, as found in the fiction of William Styron's *Sophie's Choice* or Shakespeare's *Romeo and Juliet* or in the non-fictional choice of Gudrun Ensslin of the Red Army Faction to end her life. Repeating the choice takes on another dimension when Kierkegaard and Walter Benjamin are brought into play to explore how a past event can be repeated and reclaimed from the dead weight of history. Repeating October 1917, for example, would mean releasing possibilities stifled by the course history took and not realized at the time.

The chapter continues with a fairly dense excursion into Hegelian dialectics (pp. 97–102), the point of which is to assert the paradox pertaining to identity: it being upheld by a feature which contradicts its own terms of reference. An example given is the way in which a state, claiming a rational wholeness, rests on a monarch who is irrationally there due to an accident of birth. Identity is also authoritarian in nature and this is explored by returning to Kierkegaard and his view of the truth of Christ as resting not in what he said (the enunciated) but in the fact that it was Christ who said it (the act of enunciation). This for Žižek is the nature of authority, identity depends on it, and support for this is found in types of speech that bring about a state of affairs by stating something to be the case (as in 'I declare this meeting closed'). Ontological reality is brought about by language in its purely performative dimension, although this is masked by the symbolic network which relies on the opposite, constative, assertion that reality is an already given. The Master Signifier, transcendental, self-founding and authoritarian, is positioned at the crossroad of the performative and the constative and is able to quilt and totalize the necessarily open field of signifiers by taking the place of that lack which always escapes the structure. Chapter Three draws to an end by explicating the role of the Lacanian psychoanalyst in terms of suspending the regime of the Master Signifier and repeating the forced choice by bringing this signifier into the open. In the same spirit, an 'act' suspends the operation of the symbolic order and repeats the forced choice so as to allow for a different outcome.

Highbrow Lacanian analyses, orbiting around *jouissance* and the Thing, characterize the next chapter. The theme of the monster, whether in Munch's *Scream*, David Lynch films or the tale of Kasper Hauser, is related to the subject's troubling encounter with its own negative, the Thing that marks the very void that lies at the heart of the subject. Readers with an interest in film studies might be tempted to skip to the first section of Chapter five for its detailed analysis of *film noir* and the book's last chapter for what it says about Hitchcock. The motifs traced in Hitchcock's films are not interpreted as narrative devices or archetypal symbols, they essentially have no meaning, but the libidinal force they express makes them akin to the Lacanian *sinthome* and they define that element of the Hitchcock aura that unsettles an audience by drawing it towards some preontological abyss. Another aspect of the Hitchcock universe is his employment of the need for the gaze of the Other, exemplified by the shot of the dying detective in *Psycho* or the frame of Bodega Bay as seen by the birds in *The Birds*. Staying in the cinema, *Enjoy Your Symptom!* concludes by looking at *The Matrix* and develops some neat (re)elaborations of the big Other and the real in the process of outlining the film's philosophical and psychoanalytic inconsistencies.

TARRYING WITH THE NEGATIVE (1993)

Two films, *Angel Heart* and *Blade Runner*, provide the book's kick-start but the reader is soon required to follow some intricate philosophical footwork around Kant and then Hegel and Lacan. Žižek finds the Lacanian decentered subject in Kant's 'I of apperception', though Kant was not prepared to follow through the radical implications of his thought and hence ambiguities and inconsistencies with the I of apperception, the noumenal self and the transcendental object. These ambiguities are viewed as 'a necessary equivocality' if Kantian theory is to hold together:[7] there cannot be a noumenal Self that appears to itself as a phenomenon because this would collapse the noumenon/phenomenon distinction; but if there is no noumenal Self then the distinction again collapses, this time into a Hegelian self-positing of presuppositions. While Hegel's bringing together of substance and subject looks like the polar opposite of the Kantian gap between the Thing-in-itself of substance and the I of the subject, Žižek prefers to formulate the union as a preservation of the gap but in a negative manner; in this mode the Thing-in-itself becomes a content-less abyss.

Žižek wants to defend and build upon what might seem like difficulties in Kant and, similarly, he wants to defend Hegel against misrepresentations (including ones coming from Marx) that hinge on a failure to see how the Hegelian subject relates to a split in substance. This, via Kant's transcendental object, leads to the role and nature of *objet petit a*. The transcendental object is a concept of the object, not derived from experience, that allows the object to be distinct from our representation of it. This concept does not point to an object that is purely external or substantial; it is a necessary concept that allows for, points towards, the possibility of objectivity. It conceives of the object as 'non-empirical' and 'only as something in general = x'.[8] It is tempting to equate the transcendental object with the thing-in-itself because they are alike in their unknowableness and the way they both underlie appearances but while the transcendental object allows us to think of the thing-in-itself it does not originate from it. It is ontologically empty and not to be confused with the epistemological inaccessibility of the thing-in-itself. It is the ground of appearance but, as Žižek puts it, 'conceived of in the mode of our thinking' because the transcendental object has to be thought of if there is to be a consistency to our experience.[9] The point Žižek is arguing towards is that the transcendental object conceived of in this way opens the way, regrettably, for the inaccessible x to acquire substantiality; and the homologue to this is the Real thought of as the thing-in-itself and *objet petit a* as the transcendental object. What would be melodrama to anyone but an impassioned philosopher, Žižek states: 'It is here that the fate of our comprehension of Lacan and Kant is decided':[10] the point that is crucial for a proper comprehension being the error of allowing *objet a* to invoke the mirage of a substantial Real and, correlatively, failing to see that the Kantian thing-in-itself is also a illusion, invoked in its case by the transcendental object.

Chapter Two turns to Kant *avec* Lacan by forcing the concept of the sublime to reveal possibilities Kant preferred not to consider and modelling a correspondence between Kant's antinomies and Lacanian sexual difference. The modelling, a fine example of Žižek's addiction to theory, might uncharitably be described as embroidering and some readers – relieved when the account turns to the film *It's a Wonderful Life* and a dream case of Freud's to illustrate points previously formulated in dense Lacanese – may feel they are being told more about Lacan than they wish to know. The moral of the exercise is to see how Lacan interprets pathological mental states such as hysteria or compulsive neurosis as ways of designating 'existential-ontological positions'.[11] So, for example, the neurotic who clings to his compulsive disorder or the Kantian moral subject questioning the motives for his behaviour is practising something akin to Cartesian doubt and seeking a grounding for self-belief, a balm for the anxiety-inducing uncertainty of not knowing what I am for the desire of the Other, what in me counts as *objet petit a* for the Other's desire (illustrated by Žižek in the ending of Hitchcock's *Suspicion*). For the hysteric or pervert this need takes on an urgency that renders them clinically ill while for others anxiety can be assuaged by ideological signifiers of the 'I believe in x' kind which 'mean that I believe that I am not alone, that I believe that there are others who believe in x'.[12] But this x, like the Name-of-the-Father, is ultimately a signifier for the lack of identity and a means of consecrating *loss*.

The fine-tuning and philosophical refining of Lacanian ideas continue in Chapter Three with a gnomic proposition from *Ecrits* that 'speech is able to recover the debt that it engenders'. An understanding of this pertains to the paradox of 'symbolic fictions' (Žižek's term here for Kant's 'regulative ideas'): they provide access to reality but also occlude it and if abandoned reality disperses. This is the dialectical form of the symbolic order. The 'debt' in the Lacanian statement is the sacrifice the subject has to make for entry to the symbolic order of language. This is not so much the familiar idea found in Freud's example of the child who plays with a spool, throwing it out of sight and recovering it, repeating *fort* (away)/*da* (here) as a means of symbolizing the mother who is no longer always present and the consequent anguish of experiencing severance from a whole love, but more the idea from Hegel of the word as murder of the thing – 'The first act, by which Adam established his lordship over the animals, is this, that he gave them a name, i.e., he nullified them as beings on their own account'[13] – the mortification that comes from naming, replacing the thing itself with its name, is the price paid for the thing's representation in the word (the death drive can be seen as the drive for what is beyond representation).[14] Lacanian thought equates the 'debt' with the wound of losing not just the mother but a part of the subject's being that is sacrificed when I am no longer an object of the other's desire and become instead the grammatical 'I' of discourse, the subject of the enunciated. The 'recovery' that Lacan refers to comes about because language, before serving as a means of communication, operates primarily like a password, serving to allow entry into a particular symbolic space, the social nexus. The enunciated content, like the words of a chosen password, has a arbitrariness that makes it 'empty' but this voidness is necessary for subjects' mutual recognition.[15] This is the recovery and, like Kant's regulative ideas, what is necessary for the functioning of a consistent reality is at the same time, paradoxically, a negative dismembering of an organic whole.

It is the dialectical movement that interests Žižek and, in a bold move, he discerns it at work again in the way Kant's notion of 'radical evil' (a self-incurring, a priori propensity to evil) opens the space for, is prior to, Good. Going further, the notion is equated with the death drive and its negative breaking up of the substantial Whole, a fracturing of the organic completeness that allows for Good to transpire. This is how the dialectic works, not a self-mediation but the emergence of a new totality from a subordinated moment of what existed before. Žižek then returns to the antinomies and looks at Kant's distinction between negative and indefinite judgements as a way of clarifying the phenomenon/noumenon distinction. The last section of this chapter (pp. 119–24) perspicuously draws out the dialectical logic that accounts for the emergence of *objet petit a* as the result of the sublation (Hegel's *Aufhebung*) of need by desire. The opening of Hegel's *Science of Logic*, with the passage of Being into Nothing, demonstrates the logic at work:

> Let us take a moment X: all attempts to grasp its concealed essence, to determine it more concretely, end in failure, and the subsequent moment only positivizes this failure; in it failure as such assumes positive existence. In short, one fails to determine the truth of X, and this failure is the truth of X.[16]

Such a passage is traced by Žižek in the Lacanian triad of *need-demand-desire* using the example of how an infant's need for a drink provides a medium for the expression of a demand for the mother's love (analogous to the way Marx sees capitalism as a medium in which the use-value of a worker's labour functions as exchange-value under the form of the commodity). The need is posited, presupposed rather than experienced as a particular need, because within the symbolic space that is the Lacanian context here what matters is the call to an Other, in this example the infant's cry to the mother, for testimony of love. A deadlock is reached because meeting the need cannot meet the demand, and the failure is resolved, synthesized, in the negation of the negation that positivizes, embodies, the loss by appeasably producing the *objet petit a*. What is continually stressed by Žižek is the fallacy of seeing the Hegelian synthesis as a symphony, there is no harmonious completion only a symbolic appeasement that affirms and acknowledges the lack by giving it an identity. The mistake of thinking otherwise would be like reporting as missing to the police one's lost virginity, hopelessly confusing something material with a yearning for something that never was what it is now taken to be, as if absence necessarily carries with it a previous presence.

The next chapter, 'Hegel's "Logic of Essence" as a Theory of Ideology', in its acute exposition of the nature and applicability of the dialectic, forms the philosophical nucleus of *Tarrying with the Negative*. A lot of Hegelian territory is covered, moving at pace from the 'in-itself/for-itself', the three types of reflection, the thing's 'return to itself', the meshing of contingency and necessity, and using a rich variety of examples: the difference between Kant and Hegel in their treatment of existence (opposing the logic of Kant's argument against the ontological proof of God to the Hegelian movement in Marx's depiction of how the proletarian becomes revolutionary through a self-referential realignment of his subject position), racism, the Renaissance's discovery of antiquity, the movie *Jaws*, Kant's transcendental object. What is being driven home is that necessity is not some essence but a contingency that bears witness to the ontological incompleteness of reality. A 'necessity' that can be discerned is the compulsion to think there is an indispensability behind the veil of appearance, like the anti-Semite who sees behind the economic and social imbalance the requisite essence that substantializes itself as the 'Jewish plot'. What there is, for Žižek as for Hegel, is 'the dialectical unity of actual and possible', a convergence between subject and object wherein the only meaningful distinction is a formal one of different modalities:[17] in the mode of subjectivity there is only pure, restless, open becoming while in the mode of objectivity, uniting subject and object in being, there is necessity. The error in much philosophy is to take one mode to the exclusion of the other and render the one-dimensionality of either a grand casual nexus or a grand existentialist freedom. Either way, what is preserved is a form of ontological unity and this is exactly what the dialectic denies.

Žižek intrepidly brings Lacan back into this discussion by conceiving of *objet petit a* as an anticipation of a form to be completed or, negatively, as something lost, a form that never completed itself. This, opposing an orthodox reading in which 'the telos of the dialectical process is the absolute form that abolishes any material surplus', produces instead a reading whereby 'Hegel conceives of matter as correlative to incomplete form'.[18]

Is not the crucial shift in a dialectical process the reversal of anticipation – not into its fulfilment, but – into retroaction? If, therefore, the fulfilment never occurs in the Present, does this not testify to the irreducible status of *objet a*?[19]

After this daring combination of Hegel and Lacan, the remainder of *Tarrying with the Negative* is like a set of gentle cooling down exercises after vigorous exertion.

THE METASTASES OF ENJOYMENT (1994)

This book begins with a dense summary of how cultural critics, the Frankfurt School in particular, have read Freudian psychoanalysis, with Žižek saving his ire for the failure of Habermas to see beyond the 'latent dream-thought' to the trauma of the Real in the unconscious, a trauma that cannot be reduced to a hermeneutic anchored in the language of intersubjective communication. Chapter Two develops the paradoxical logic of time in Freudian analysis whereby the traumatic cause, as the result of being attached to some present deadlock, is retrospectively posited. The Lacanian subject is then located in the same disjunction that arises in the Real.

The third chapter begins with examples using a movie (*A Few Good Men*) and the Ku Klux Klan of unofficially sanctioned transgressions hidden from public law and ends with the case of the skinhead who in the privacy of his home is kind and considerate yet in public brutally abuses and attacks immigrants. Although one seems to be an inversion of the other they are not dissimilar and a Greimasian semiotic square is used to model the positions of ethics and morality in their common psychic field, called the superego by Freud. In what are perhaps the most compelling sections of this chapter (pp. 73–82), there are reflections on what can happen when the space for symbolic fiction is suffocated by an aestheticized reality and the terrible consequences, in extreme cases, of exposing the *objet a* that cocoons the empty core of our being. Traversing the fantasy, confronting the myths that sustain symbolic worlds, becomes an ethical obligation when the cruel penalties of not doing are clear to see.

A favoured example of Lacan's for the *petit objet a* is the tradition of courtly love, where endless postponements are the point and not the problem: the hindrances that prevent the knight from reaching the lady function as obstacles created in order to sustain the illusion that if only they could be overcome the object of the quest would be reached. Žižek devotes a chapter to this topic, exploring its variations mainly through films, and offers an appealing account of how Neil Jordan's *The Crying Game* touches the nature of authentic love. Film analysis continues with a reading of Lynch's *Blue Velvet* before shifting to the philosopher Deleuze, bringing the reader closer to the subject matter of the book's subtitle, *On Women and Causality*. The sustained misogyny of Otto Weininger's *Sex and Character* is seen as expressing a fear of the void at the heart of subjectivity, an hysterical fear that can be seen as ultimately responsible for his suicide in his early twenties.

The appendix to *The Metastases of Enjoyment* takes the form of a self-interview which is far from being a narcissistic exercise. Žižek asks himself why examples from popular culture populate his work, what exactly is the nature of *objet petit a* and of the link between Hegel and Lacan, and between Derrida and Lacan, and why a psychoanalytic approach is vital to an understanding of the world we inhabit.

THE INDIVISIBLE REMAINDER (1996) AND THE ABYSS OF FREEDOM (1997)

First published in 1996, with a new edition in 2007, *The Indivisible Remainder* is a reading of Schelling's esoteric theosophy as a metaphor or allegory for the genesis of subjectivity. *The Indivisible Remainder* is the most difficult to read and boldly speculative of all Žižek's books and this is due to the sheer complexity of the subject matter and the fact that most readers will not be familiar with Schelling's philosophy – notwithstanding Terry Eagleton's observation in 1997 that 'over the past few years [Schelling] has been shot from Teutonic obscurity to something like philosophical stardom'.[20]

One advantage of the other book about Schelling, *The Abyss of Freedom*, is that Žižek's text, taking up more than half of the book's 182 pages, is an extended introduction to Schelling's second draft of *Die Weltalter* (*Ages of the World*) and a translation of this work by Judith Norman follows the introduction. *The Abyss of Freedom* is best read before *The Indivisible Remainder* because in it there is a cogent explanation of how Schelling's account of the transition from Ground to Existence relates to Lacan's formulations of the barred subject.[21]

Žižek has also contributed an essay in a book about Schelling, 'Everything You Wanted to Know About Schelling (But Were Afraid to Ask Hitchcock)' and it serves as a user-friendly way of understanding why the German philosopher is held in such high regard by Žižek.[22] The essay concerns versions of the Real in Schelling and how motifs in Hitchcock's films can be seen to render these ideas of reality as virtual and incomplete. There is a scene in *Shadow of a Doubt* when the young Charlie is taken out by an FBI detective, without realizing his identity, and they are walking down the street engaged in innocuous conversation when an unexpected fade out occurs and gives way to the astonished gaze of Charlie and her utterance, 'I know who you are really! You are a detective!' Only *after* this moment does the detective explain his suspicions about her uncle. Žižek reads the gaze of Charlie as a precipitation of the event (the detective's rationale), a reversal of cause and effect that announces a break in the normally uninterrupted texture of reality. Such a break is a signal of the Real, the gaze opens up the ontological plasticity that is the Ground in Schelling's theosophy and for Žižek Schelling is the first philosopher to give a coherent account of this spectral realm of the pre-ontological.

Adrian Johnston devotes a significant part of his *Žižek's Ontology* (2008) to Schelling (pp. 69–122), believing as he does that the philosopher's importance has been eclipsed by Hegel and that Schelling 'plays an absolutely pivotal role in the overall structure of the Žižekian theoretical matrix'[23]; as a supplement and an aid to reading *The Indivisible Remainder* and *The Abyss of Freedom*, Johnston's account can be recommended.

THE PLAGUE OF FANTASIES (1997)

In Žižek's preface to the new 2008 edition the focus of *The Plague of Fantasies* is said to be 'the twisted topology' of *objet petit a*; a suitable term given the challenge presented for any unwary orienteer who approaches this terrain unequipped with the necessary theoretical kit. The first chapter, exploring how fantasy works at an ideological level, is not the easiest way into the book, and readers might benefit from starting with the compelling account of *jouissance* that opens Chapter Two. The concept is brought to life with examples from everyday life and *film noir* before using it to bring out the insight and the limitations of Goldhagen's thesis in *Hitler's Willing Executioners* (that the Holocaust was carried out not be psychopaths but by ordinary Germans raised in a deeply anti-Semitic culture), and the difference between Nazism and Stalinism.

The third chapter, 'Fetishism and its Vicissitudes', weaves a complex model of subjectivity that packs in ideas and patterns in a heady, typically Žižekian manner. It gets underway with Hegel's dialectic (pp. 116–20) before turning to Marx's commodity fetishism, expanding its scope and significance by way of Lacan. People act as if unaware of the substitution of things for people in commodity fetishism, behaviour that cannot be understood without seeing 'the subject supposed to believe' as lying at the heart of the big Other. Belief has an inherent reflectivity, i.e. others can believe for me, I can believe through others, and it can operate without there being some subjectively present person really existing and directly believing. This substitution works with different fetish-things – canned laughter in TV sit-coms, Tibetan prayer wheels, women hired to cry at funerals – as material forms of the substitution of a signifier for the subject. It is in this way that the barred subject is created, through the big Other as a substitution for the Real, because there is no substantial core to the subject – and the void, the passivity of its Being, can be filled by the Other. One's *jouissance*, embodied in the fetish, can be transposed to the Other – a displacement Žižek here calls interpassivity – and this disavowal of one's core passivity allows one to get on with living: 'if I am to function as pure activity, I have to externalize my (passive) Being – in short: I have to be passive *through another*' (p. 152). Thus the fetishist object is *objet petit a* and the operation of fantasy can be described as 'objectively subjective' (p. 158): really there but inaccessible to the subject's self-experience.

After an interesting analysis of a group of Buñuel films, Chapter Four examines virtual reality and cyberspace in psychoanalytic terms. Žižek sets up the necessary context for his critical view with filmic examples – the actual and possible endings of Capra's *Meet John Doe* and Hitchcock's *Notorious* – to show how the phantasmic support underlying a social reality can be seen as a form of hypertext. Cyberspace is different because it can actualize different endings or beginnings, as well as everything in between, and the implications of this are what interest Žižek. What if we get to see what happened to Heathcliff in the three years he was away from Wuthering Heights? What if the unspoken in a Henry James novel is rendered explicit? With everything open to choice and nothing remaining unsaid, something vital is lost. The symbolic surface depends on there being a space, a gap, between itself and the fantasy that supports it; if everything is virtualized and made excessively present the delicate balance between our symbolic selves and a poised presence of the Real is broken.

The first of the book's three appendices is an easy-going look at ways of representing the sexual act in some Hollywood movies while the second is a Lacanian-inspired reading of Schumann's songs and piano pieces. The final appendix, considering the nature of an ethics founded on the real, is a fairly condensed account and assumes some knowledge of Kantian ethics on the part of the reader. Not for the philosophically faint-hearted but an invigorating end to a book fuelled by the energy of ideas and scholarship.

THE TICKLISH SUBJECT (1999)

Announcing its intent on the first page with a pastiche of the opening to the *Communist Manifesto*, this book sets out to rescue the notion of subjectivity first propounded by Descartes and save it from the various forms of attack (which can be labelled as the forces of anti-Cartesianism) that would reduce the subject to merely an array of historically situated identities (cultural, ethnic, sexual and so on). There is, it will be stoutly argued, a kernel of the self but it is not some Kantian noumenal core and nor can it be merged with the body and brain. *The Ticklish Subject* is a substantial and original work of philosophy that sets out a consistent account of subjectivity with the help of Lacan and Hegel. It starts with Žižek's high regard for Heidegger and the desire to locate where he went wrong without falling into the trap of branding his error as irrationalism and a blind decisionism. What Žižek finds in Heidegger to endorse is the utter groundlessness to our existence and the resoluteness with which the individual 'chooses' a life, a tradition – a choice that is not really free (as if all options were openly available to us) because our destiny is there before us but, nonetheless, we have to choose it (like the Lacanian 'forced choice').[24] Heidegger is credited with recognizing in Kant a dimension of radical subjectivity but then withdrawing himself from the challenge of following it through, turning to Nazism as an escape route. This first chapter is important for an appreciation of how Žižek's philosophy develops out of his engagement with German Idealism.

In the account of Kant's 'transcendental turn' given earlier there was a role for the synthesis of imagination in the process of cognition (p. 50) but in Heidegger's reading this role takes on an importance that is only ambivalently present in Kant; imagination becomes capable of being analysed in its own right but such a step was avoided by Kant because of the radically unsettling implications it would entail. Žižek seizes on Heidegger's insight and sees Kant as avoiding not the synthetic power of imagination but its opposite, the negative power to break down what was previously a whole. In *The Ticklish Subject* Žižek aligns such a negative capability with what Hegel described in his 'night of the world' passage and in this way the notion of negation 'is thus transcendental imagination at its most elementary and violent ... which dissolves every objective link, every connection grounded in the thing itself'.[25] Although Kant avoided taking such a step himself, he introduced the possibility of antagonism between imagination and understanding and in doing so located the place of the Real:

> The pre-synthetic Real, its pure, not-yet-fashioned 'multitude' not yet synthesized by a minimum of transcendental imagination, is, *stricto sensu, impossible*: a level that must be retroactively presupposed, but can never actually be *encountered*.[26]

This for Žižek is Kant's tremendous importance and he interprets the Kantian sublime in the light of this ontological break that the German philosopher made possible. The sublime draws attention to the fact that transcendental imagination cannot realize a closed, consistently whole cosmos (because such a cosmos is not there) – 'the Sublime confronts us with the failure of imagination, with that which remains forever and a priori un-imaginable – and it is here that we encounter the subject *qua* the void of negativity'[27] – and Heidegger's omission of a discussion of the sublime in his reading of Kant becomes symptomatic of the way he shunned the excess and madness that inheres to such a dimension of subjectivity. This, argues Žižek, is what allows for a soft rendition of Heidegger's 'being-in-the-world' as a realm without the autonomous subject, just layers of 'embeddedness' making up the life-world we happen to be 'thrown' into as finite, existential beings, with the Freudian unconscious as a part of this opaque background into which we are rooted. Opposing this is Žižek's employment of the unconscious as the Hegelian 'night of the world' and the Lacanian death drive, the void of subjectivity that ruptures the engaged immersion that is being-in-the-world. The rupture *is* the subject and is outside of the temporality that becomes for Heidegger the crucial horizon making up the experience of Being. The first chapter of *The Ticklish Subject* comes to an end by asking what is the connection between this rupture and the 'anxiety' that Heidegger describes in *Being and* Time (1985), the not-being-at-home experience that so disturbs *Dasein*.

In the first section of Chapter Two (pp. 70–5) there is a summary of the dialectic, emphasizing repetition and redoubling in the negation of negation and finding examples in a New Age book, Slovenian politics and a breakdown in a couple's relationship. The chapter goes on to explain the complexity of the rapport between Substance and Subject via Lacan's anamorphosis and a delving into deep Hegelian matters: the structure of *Science of Logic* and 'concrete' and 'abstract' universality. At the beginning and end of the 'Concrete Universality' section (pp. 98–103), Žižek states the point he is coming to: the dialectic that *Science of Logic* presents, the process whereby every category contains its opposite:

> ... far from signalling the failure of our thought to grasp reality, the inherent inconsistency of our notional apparatus is the ultimate proof that our thought is not merely a logical game we play, but is able to reach reality itself, expressing its inherent structuring principle.[28]

And what is this principle?

> The Hegelian 'concrete universality' thus involves the Real of some central impossibility: universality is 'concrete', structured as a texture of particular figurations, precisely because it is forever prevented from acquiring a figure that would be adequate to its notion. This is why – as Hegel puts it – the Universal genus is always *one of its own species*: there is universality only in so far as there is a gap, a hole, in the midst of the particular content of the universality in question, that is, in so far as, among the species of a genus, there is always one species missing: namely, the species that would adequately embody the genus itself.[29]

Žižek details an example of this in the concept of the violin

concerto and the remainder of this chapter produces other interesting examples, like the appeal of Latin as opposed to Greek and
the ascetic's self-discipline to illustrate Hegelian and Lacanian ideas.
Whereas the first chapter of *The Ticklish Subject* assumes an
acquaintance with Kant and Heidegger and the second does the
same for Hegel, the third chapter starts with Alain Badiou but as his
book, *Being and Event* (2007), had not at the time been translated
into English Žižek does not take for granted the reader's familiarity
with his key ideas. Consequently, there is a useful presentation
of these ideas (pp. 128–41) before subjecting them to a critical
commentary. There is an obvious similarity between Badiou's Event
and Žižek's act, and they will come to share an interest in the
importance of St Paul that obviates any need to actually believe in
something like the Resurrection, but Žižek wants more space for
psychoanalysis than Badiou is willing to allow. Death for Badiou
is just a terminal, undialectical point before the Truth-Event of
the Resurrection – one is not mediated by the other – but Žižek
sees Death as the negative moment of withdrawal that dialectically
makes Resurrection possible, the 'indivisible remainder' that belongs
to the core of subjectivity, an excremental excess from which traditional humanism shies away. This is a way of saying that Žižek wants
to insist on the full force of a Lacanian understanding of the subject
– the subject as the negation that is Hegel's night of the world and
which creates the space for subjectivization – and not just a process
of subjectivization that emerges from an Event and bestow on it
its fidelity. This distinction is carefully set out and defended in the
section 'The Lacanian Subject' (pp. 158–61). The next chapter then
looks at the forms of subjectivization in the political philosophies of
Laclau, Rancière and Balibar.

Chapter Five gets into gear with an outline of the psychoanalytic difference between perversion and hysteria: the pervert,
lacking nothing bar lack itself, thinks he knows what enjoyment
consists of while the hysteric questions and doubts what desire is
wanting or asking; perversion suits our 'post-ideological' age and
its enthrallment to the superego's injunction to enjoy but hysteria
has a subversive potential. Žižek then turns to Foucault and how his
accounts of disciplining sexuality fail to include the erotic charge that
enmeshes itself into the mechanisms of repression. This form of self-
referentiality is properly Hegelian and it can model other categories
of experience, as when national identity emerges as a result of, is

contained within, colonial domination. It also points to an internal excess, an inbuilt inconsistency that can prove self-detonating, all of which is a way of describing subjectivity (the dimension that is seen to be missing from Foucault). This then leads to a discussion of how the existing order of power relations, sets of 'symbolic norms *and* their codified transgressions'[30], can be effectively undermined. The only way of doing this is by undoing the 'fundamental fantasy' that sustains a subject's being and such a traversal involves 'subjective destitution' and not just the kind of tinkering with symbolic forms of attachment (an example (p. 266) of such a tinkering being the progressive reworking to the series of *Dirty Harry* films). This referencing to Lacanian ideas also informs Žižek's engagement with the philosopher Judith Butler about sexual difference and his defence of a Lacanian approach to sexuality with the help of an example from Hitchcock's *Vertigo* (pp. 286–7). This film is also referenced in what is the best part of this chapter, the 'From Desire to Drive ... and Back' section (pp. 290–306), dealing with the paradox of drive, its reflexive turn that revolves the 'I' into the abhorrent Thing which cannot be identified with, and the congruence of this psychoanalytic understanding with the philosophy of German Idealism.

The Ticklish Subject concludes by coming down from a theoretical stratosphere to politically focused ground, to the 'post-Oedipal' subject of the world we now inhabit. The waning of a paternal authority that once gave substance to social being gives rise to new issues of identity vis-à-vis the big Other. The dilution in the efficiency of symbolic fictions has reached a point where ethical committees are needed to makes new rules for areas of life that have arisen from, for example, advances in the science of genetics. One result of this is anxiety at not having some 'infallible' tradition that provided Knowledge, reduces us all to a figure like the unwitting Forrest Gump (p. 338). What is needed is a leap of faith that can provide the essential ground of trust and the ability offered by psychoanalysis to identify and resist the new forms of subjection to a depoliticized Capital that thrives on the plethora of contingent identities masking an underlying ideology. There are novel props that seek to reassert a felt sense of the big Other, like the penchant for conspiracy theories that all-purposively can serve the traditional left as well as the right (p. 362). The irony for an age supposedly liberated from old forms of patriarchy and sexual repression is that 'the direct injunction [of the superego] "Enjoy!" is a much more effective way to hinder the subject's access to enjoyment than the explicit Prohibition which sustains the space for its transgression'.[31] Žižek sees one result of this in the way more libidinal energy goes into preparing and presenting one's sexuality than is ultimately derived from the sexual experience itself. This need to find a mark of the Real is also used by Žižek to weave a theory about the liking for mutilating the body through tattoos and piercing and how this is the opposite of traditional body markings like circumcision. This becomes one instance of what Žižek is tempted to call the antinomies of postmodern individuality: constant self-fashioning of identity only draws attention to an anxiety-inducing lack of identity. Such instances draw attention to the importance of psychoanalysis: the need for an act and the traversing of the fantasy that supports 'idle' activities.

THE FRIGHT OF REAL TEARS (2001)

Subtitled *Krzysztof Kieślowski between Theory and Post-theory*, this book intervenes in film theory debates that were current at the time of its publication (the text is made up of lectures delivered in London in 1998) and while it will appeal most obviously to students and scholars of film studies the application of Lacanian ideas to the work of film directors, principally though not only Krzysztof Kieślowski, will be of interest to a far wider audience. Reality is 'not all' and to deal with this ontological puzzle some parts of it have to be experienced as spectral and 'sutured'. The scene from *Possessed* where Joan Crawford gazes up at a passing train (also used in *The Pervert's Guide to the Cinema*) and the scene from *The Double Life of Véronique* where Véronique sits at a train window are used to show how cinema can realize a spectral magic within drab reality, as opposed to reality being reduced to a spectre as in the close-up of Julie's eye, with the doctor a mere reflection within it, after the car accident in Kieślowski's *Blue*. This shot from *Blue* is referred to again towards the end of the book, contrasting it with the film's final scene, to show the movement from Julie's willed withdrawal-into-self and her derealizing of others to the epiphanic moment, where the camera drifts in one long shot between the four people she has accepted into her life, when she is symbolically reborn. A close-up of Julie's eye completes the long shot but unlike the moment in the hospital scene it no longer reflects apparitions, as in Hegel's 'night of the world', but becomes instead 'the locus of the reconstructed fantasy through which the subject regains access to reality'.[32] The car accident that killed her husband and child also killed the frame of fantasy within which her life made sense and she confronted the Real of her loss and the Real of raw life that she was left with. The film's movement does not chart the human process of coming to terms with reality but the rebuilding of fantasy's protective screen that allows social life to resume its normal pattern.[33]

Another example of the cinematic rendering of Lacanian ideas comes from the pathological adherence of Kane in *Citizen Kane* to his *objet petit a* and the wide-lens effect that accentuates the gap between the 'immature' stubbornness of his subjectivity and the objectivity of his public environment. In Minghella's *The Talented Mr Ripley*, on the other hand, the film provides psychological fill-ins for what is not explored in Patricia Highsmith's novel of the same name and in this way partly erases the very void of subjectivity in Ripley that makes him such a deeply disturbing character. To appreciate most of Žižek's examples it helps to have seen Kieślowski's *The Decalogue* (1988), *The Double Life of Véronique* (1990) and the trilogy *Three Colors* (1993–4) but synopses are given and anyone new to the films is likely to want to seek them out after reading this book.

In the book's 'Introduction' (pp. 5–6), Žižek tells how he once bluffed his way through an arts discussion, in relation to a painting he was asked to comment on but one which he had never seen before, by spinning a theoretical tale about the invisible gap between different frames. To his surprise, his vacuous chatter was received with the utmost seriousness; the apparent moral of this tale being the pseudo intellectualism of much that passes for cultural studies. But later in the book (p. 130), discussing features of Kieślowski's films, Žižek uses the very same text with absolutely no indication that he is being ironic, referring to an invisible gap between different frames as an ostensibly sober observation worth making. It might be thought that Žižek is parodying himself or engaging in an academic prank were it not that five years later in *The Parallax View* the same text is used yet again as part of a serious account of how the notion of parallax can be used to read Hegel and the nature of the Real.[34] Perhaps the sense that can be attached to his account of the bluff is the way his fellow panel members seized upon a piece of vacant theorizing in the spirit of the 'apathy at the very heart of today's cultural studies' (p. 6) as opposed to Žižek's later references to the gap between frames in *The Fright of Real Tears* and in *The Parallax*

View when he is using the idea to say something focused about specific paintings by Malevich, Hopper and Munch.

Žižek is certainly in a playful mood when he develops an amusing riff (pp. 204–5) on the history of philosophy via Lacan's maxim that 'there is no sexual relationship': starting with Descartes' 'I fuck, therefore I am' and proceeding to Spinoza's 'Absolute as Fuck', Humean doubts whether a fuck really exists when all that is given are certain apparently co-ordinated movements, Kant's transcendental fuck as opposed to Fichte's self-positing one, Hegel's insistence that fuck be conceived as Substance and Subject and Marx's ideological take on this, Nietzsche's 'Will to Fuck', and Heidegger's insight into confusion between an ontic fuck and the ontological fuck up we are thrown into.

ON BELIEF (2001)

On Belief is eloquent testimony to the author's irresistible urge to practise theory, to boldly go where no psychoanalyst has gone before. The territory to be explored is new in that it belongs to a world where capitalism can solicit and market transgression in ways never previously dared. The proliferation of sexual gadgets and toys that first create and then offer to satisfy illicit desires provides Žižek with an example of the way in which *objets a* come in the form of little packets of substitute *jouissance,* semblances of the real thing, and the question posed is whether a conversation between psychoanalysis and anti-capitalism is possible. A critic such as Badiou is inclined to say that Lacan leads to a resigned conservatism but by way of riposte *On Belief* kicks off by using psychoanalysis to expose the ideology of Western Buddhism. It operates in the form of a fetish – the embodiment of something disavowed – by allowing its believers to happily function within capitalism by allowing them to mistakenly think they are not really caught up in its soulless logic. The appeal of Western Buddhism also relates to the role of Tibet for Westerners, the place where the lost object-cause of desire is to be found, the exotic location of an ultimate spiritual wisdom. Žižek brings into this frame, via films such as *Beau Geste* and *Enigma*, the idea of sacrifice and relates it to Madame de Lafayette's *The Princess de Clèves* and, more briefly, Henry James' *The Portrait of a Lady*.

On Belief presents a cerebrally audacious interpretation of Christ that leads to the tracing of a symmetry between tragedy/comedy and desire/drive and an explication of the Judeo-Christian experience as 'grounded in a traumatic encounter of a radical Otherness'.[35] It reacts against the encounter with the Neighbour as the abyssal Thing and suggests that, like Lenin, Christianity establishes a new set of coordinates that radically redefine what is possible. Its revolutionary force resides in its traversing of whatever fantasy frames our present set of meanings, undoing our most grounded beliefs and offering a new beginning by reinventing ourselves.

It is worth noting that *On Belief* signals the significant development in Žižek's understanding of the Real, picturing it not just as primordial and inchoate but as the 'grimace' of reality, illustrated here using Lubitsch's *To Be or Not to Be* and Hitchcock's *Vertigo*, that expands from the Lacanian Real to include that which 'introduces a self-division into an ordinary object, so that the sublime dimension shines through it'.[36]

DID SOMEBODY SAY TOTALITARIANISM? (2001)

The consistency of enjoyment in starting to read this book, published in the same year as *On Belief*, may stutter a little for some readers if the quietly stated links between the opening sections are not given due attention. Modernism and postmodernism are contrasted by way of the role of myth and it is an aspect of ritual that occasions the shift to the perverse nature of desire as exemplified in the figure of the Miser (pp. 40-41). Under capitalism the same logic takes a reverse form, papering over the excess of consumption by way of the same impulse for thrift in the form of discounts, buy two and get one free offers and suchlike. This disguise of consumption behind the appearance of thrift is linked with the quid pro quo logic of ritual whereby something is sacrificed in return for something else that is wanted. This introduces the radical theology behind Christ's sacrifice for our sins and, repeating in a different key the view of Christianity from *On Belief*, the liberating potential of Christ's message and its decisive break with the tragic vision of the pagan world. The pagan world, like Buddhism, is seen to deny the possibility of deliverance from what is seen as the immutable order of existence and its preclusion of any new beginning.

The subject matter of chapter two, the Holocaust, is tightly focused throughout. The phenomena of the 'Muslim' ('Muselmann'),

Nazi concentration-camp slang for prisoners who though alive had resigned themselves to dying, is at the heart of Žižek's concerns. It is related to Hegel's 'night of the world' because of the muselmann's reduction to a 'zero level' of humanity that stands outside of language yet 'deprived even of animal vitality'.[37] There is a similarity with the condition that the victims of Stalin's show trials were reduced to but also an important difference and this is what leads into the next chapter. The irrationalism of Nazism was compacted into its anti-Semitism but the Stalinist purges lacked such containment; anyone could be victimized, plots were invented. The difference is accounted for by the authentic nature of the Bolshevik revolution, making the purges a symptom of a repressed truth about the betrayal of October 1917. Bolshevism created a utopian space, one which came to be filled by the horrors of Stalinism but whose emancipatory potential was never erased, and Žižek seeks to identify the value of this palimpsestic space. Treating Stalinism as just another absolute dictatorship is an instance for Žižek of the way the concept of totalitarianism can be used to hinder critical thought.

The next chapter begins by identifying melancholy in Lacanian terms as the object of desire being excessively fixated upon as something lost, to the point where the experience becomes a form of possession even after the original desire has faded and gone. This is contrasted with the thought of Derrida and Levinas which insists on the gap between desire and its object and thereby exposes their inability to allow for the *act*. Marxism for Derrida becomes a Messianic promise and for Levinas the call of the Other remains ultimately unanswerable, positions which cannot accommodate the totalitarian, unconditional fidelity that Antigone exemplifies. Such a fidelity facilitates a suspension of the big Other in favour of an ethics of the Real and the *act*. The criticism of Levinas concludes with a delightful reading of John Woo's film *Face/Off*.

The final chapter of the book begins by looking at Buddhist thought and cognitivist accounts of the mind as two ways of denying the notion of a self-identifying subject in favour of a more pluralist idea of the self as a bundle of rule-bound mental events that find expression in a dispersed set of discursive practices. A broader target of Žižek's criticism is the wider intellectual field that he labels Cultural Studies, characterized by a misguided adherence to historicist relativism that effaces more fundamental ontological and metaphysical questions. Totalitarianism, the book concludes, is not where you expect to find it but lurks waiting in various disguises.

CONVERSATIONS WITH ŽIŽEK (2004)

The discipline imposed by the question-and-answer format of this book helps make it one of the most comfortable and instructive ways to begin reading Žižek. There are five thematically arranged conversations, with focused questions and resolute responses that stick to the inquiry. As one of the blurbs on the back cover expresses it, 'Glyn Daly succeeds here in punctuating the febrile forward rush of one of the most distinctive and influential voices of our time'. As well as serving as a useful introduction to a range of theoretical interests, the book conveys a sense of Žižek's engaging personality as well as offering helpful refinements pertaining to his use of Lacanian terms.

ORGANS WITHOUT BODIES (2004)

The first part of this book is an engagement with Deleuze, arguing that his *Logic of Sense* is a better work than *Anti-Oedipus* and that he is not as anti-Hegelian and opposed to psychoanalysis as is commonly thought. What Žižek has to say in this respect will appeal primarily to readers who are acquainted with Deleuze and open to an unconventional interpretation of his work. The rest of *Organs without Bodies* takes up philosophical issues arising from advances in cognitive sciences before delving into film and, inevitably, Hitchcock. There is an in-depth analysis of scenes from *Vertigo* and shorter comments on *Fight Club*, *The Quiet American* and *Ivan the Terrible*.

THE PARALLAX VIEW (2006)

This is one of Žižek's most important books, a substantial and original work of philosophy that introduces parallax as his term for reality's short-circuit, the immanent gap that makes any notion of the One, any consistent whole, lack coincidence with itself. The term is traced in three major modes –ontology, science and politics – and amounts to a major restatement by Žižek of his theoretical priorities. This inevitably involves, at times, going over Kantian ground mapped out previously in books like *Tarrying With the Negative* but the difference is that he is now able to re-theorize what was said earlier by applying the parallax metaphor. This realignment allows the import of Hegel to emerge against the background of Kant's own magnitude and make visible how Hegel drew upon what, in draft form so to speak, was always there in Kant. It also allows Žižek to confirm his revised understanding of the Real and take it beyond Lacan by no longer seeing it as some unreachable core:

> The parallax Real is thus opposed to the standard (Lacanian) notion of the Real as that which 'always returns to its place' – as that which remains the same in all possible (symbolic) universes: the parallax Real is, rather, that which accounts for the very *multiplicity* of appearances of the same underlying Real ...[38]

The pace of this book's first chapter is fairly breathless and not for the faint-hearted, shifting from Hegel to Kant to Lacan to Marx at the drop of a theoretical concept and making few concessions to those unacquainted with the thinkers being discussed. The motif that is made explicit more than once is the need to rescue Hegel from false conceptions of his thought and in this spirit Žižek uses Lacan to drive home what is truly radical about ideas like self-consciousness. The latter is not some supreme force directing earthly affairs but more an awareness of one's social space and the assumptions about ourselves and others that arise from this, a dimension that brings in the force of the big Other and the object as a symptom in psychoanalysis. Lacanian terms are similarly used to add weight and meaning to Marx by positioning the critical difference between drive and desire in relation to capitalism (pp. 58–67).

The second chapter takes a surprising turn by tracing Hegelian veins in Kierkegaard's existentialism, initially via Nichols's film *The Graduate*, and along the way Žižek returns to his interest in the significance of the 'Muselmann', introduced earlier in *Did Somebody Say Totalitarianism?* The condition that some prisoners were reduced to in Nazi concentration camps becomes emblematic of a dimension of being that is not given its due by philosophers as different as Adorno and Levinas, though the latter is the main target of criticism when Žižek incisively suggests that it is the face of the Muselmann, akin to the hideous essence of the neighbour, that should call forth our ethical responsibility towards the Other. The limitation of Levinas is that he fails to recognize that 'inhuman' aspect of the Other that touches the Real, 'a monstrous dimension which is already minimally "gentrified", domesticated, once it is conceived in the Levinasian sense[?]'[39] The chapter draws to an end with an interpretation of Odradek, the strange little creature from Kafka's short story 'The Cares of a Family Man', as an embodiment of *jouissance*, Lacan's *lamella*; presenting Kafka as a writer who could explore what philosophers like Levinas prefer to keep at a safe distance.

The wide range of subject matter in *The Parallax View* continues with a shift from a Lacanian reading of Kafka to a Hegelian-inspired understanding of novels by Henry James. Substance, in this instance a society's ethical norms supposed to govern social life, is seen in Hegelian terms and thus no longer serving as a pre-existing, solidly functioning foundation. It is Subject, the interacting individuals and the mutuality of their ethical claims, gives substance to the ethical field. The original *3.10 to Yuma* western sets out the ethical landscape for Žižek before he settles in to a relatively close reading of James' *The Wings of the Dove* and *The Golden Bowl*.

The book's third chapter returns to Hegel, the catalyst being the episode from the *Prelude* when the young Wordsworth steals away one evening in a boat and becomes terrified by a mountain looming over the lake. Žižek's interest in this incident is not the poet's troubled conscience but the way the poetry realizes the gaze as a part of what is observed; subjectivity becomes inscribed into external reality. Hegel's conjunction of Substance and Subject is a way of saying that in a deep ontological sense the incoherence of the 'objective' world is bound up with the negativity that defines the space occupied by what we call the subject and this is what attracts Žižek here to topics as different as quantum physics and Badiou's Event. The subject's engagement accounts for the minimal but essential difference sustaining the 'parallax gap': it is the difference between organized unrest on the streets of St Petersburg being, for a neutral historian, one particular violent episode in Russia's turbulent history and, for a Bolshevik, a sublimely precious moment in the Event of October 1917; or, in the literary field, the difference that underlies the importance of the novelist Henning Mankell.[40]

Hegelian thought informs the concern with advances in cognitive science that Žižek conducts in Chapter Four of *The Parallax View*, engaging critically with the work of thinkers like Thomas Metzinger, Antonio Damasio and Daniel Dennett. Cognitivism explains consciousness as neurophysiological processes and Žižek warms especially to Metzinger's account of the theoretical notion of the Self as a representational construct, a self-modelling that is not apparent to the subject, aligning it on Žižek's part with the Hegelian union of substance with subject. The insights of cognitive science, that consciousness is the brain's awareness of a lack of a central network, of any 'self' directing what goes on in the mind, is seen as the answer to the puzzle – how and why did self-consciousness emerge? – in that the enigma is its own solution: it is the ontological incompleteness that accounts for the traumatic contracting out of reality, Hegel's 'night of the world', and (self-)consciousness is a 'natural', spontaneous form of this dislocation for humankind.[41]

Chapter Five gets underway by drawing in Heidegger and Nietzsche as philosophers who in their own ways grappled with the 'parallax real', the real that is the antagonistic gap in reality that prevents even the possibility arising of a non-perspectival observation of the object 'out there'. The necessary consequence is not relativism but the truth that *is* the distortion caused by the ontological gap and this leads to an account of why Stalinism and Nazism cannot be equated. Far from trying to diminish the horrors of Stalinism, Žižek stresses how life under that regime was subject to a deeper level of irrational violence than life under Nazi rule. A kind of 'normal' existence was possible under Hitler if you were not a Jew and remained politically passive, while Stalinism turned against its own members in a way that bore witness to its traumatic betrayal of the revolutionary endeavour inaugurated in October 1917. The Stalinist terror in its 'madness' sought to erase its authentic revolutionary origins and while dissident Communists could seek to retrieve this utopian potential any notion of 'Nazism with a human face' remains an obscene untruth. Žižek agrees with Badiou that the October Revolution was a 'Truth-Event' and Stalinism never severed its remaining link with civilization while Nazism was barbarism from beginning to end.

'So where are we today?' is the pertinent question asked after the preceding discussion.[42] The age of global capitalism has coupled surplus value with surplus enjoyment, with the begetting of profit now dependent on a constant goading of the system's own excess and, as Žižek shows by how the potential in the first film of *The Matrix* trilogy was not followed through, it is easier to analyse and present the problem than envisage a workable solution. He concurs with

Badiou that capitalism has attained a state of 'worldlessness', it does not require a cognitive roadmap because it can attach itself to very different social orders (those of China, of Muslim states, of liberal democracies and so on) and operate as a neutral, universal system, constantly reinventing itself. At his gloomiest, Žižek considers that perhaps the best one can do is expose the kind of false comforts represented in John Ford's *Fort Appache* and Clint Eastwood's *Mystic River*. Politically, this means rejecting the false choices being offered between liberalism and fundamentalism, democracy and terror, and confronting the basic class antagonism, the parallax gap in politics, that divides society. In a proper Hegelian manner, the external liberalism-fundamentalism antinomy needs to be seen as internal to the governing ideology and what needs bringing into the light is the disavowed obscene level that supplements 'normal' life, examples of which range from paedophilia within the Catholic Church to the unwritten but acceptable transgressions that a film like *A Few Good Men* reveals.

Žižek's book concludes more positively by returning to the parallax view idea via Melville's novella *Bartleby, the Scrivener: A Story of Wall Street*, a tale of withdrawal from the world and the titular character's response to every request, 'I would prefer not to'. This is not the negation of a predicate ('I don't prefer to ...') but the positive affirmation of a non-predicate; politically, it translates into passive aggression not quietist indifference, instead of a preliminary clearing of the decks it is the fixing of a new political space. Most importantly, it is not a Buddhist-like withdrawal from desire and the embrace of an inner peace distanced from illusionary reality. This is cheating, a way of working within capitalism by keeping metaphysically outside of it, a serene way of participating by, so to speak, keeping one's fingers crossed.[43] Žižek enigmatically remarks how the parallax view explains how Bartleby politics would reduce the gap between the public order of Law and its underground, obscene supplement. He goes on to unpack this a little by shifting to a philosophical plane to explain how the gap is that which exists between something and nothing, meaning that the difference in the position of an object arising from a shift in perspective, i.e. parallax, is the difference between reality and the void that is always a part of the reality. This 'non-all' is the ontological incompleteness of the world and at the political level it is the premise of Bartleby's 'I would prefer not to', an embodied negativity, a subtraction that creates the empty space for an act to take place. What this means in practice is a refusal to endorse those gestures of resistance – charities and Greenpeace-like protests and resolutions are Žižek's examples – that only oil the machinery of the prevailing system. Earlier in *The Parallax View* (pp. 81–5), the same kind of Bartleby imperative is traced in an obscure drama, Paul Claudel's *The Hostage*, and the better known act of renunciation by Isabel Archer, in Henry James' *The Portrait of a Lady*, when she refuses to leave her thoroughly nasty husband.

HOW TO READ LACAN (2006)

Each of the book's seven sections takes a short extract from Lacan's work and proceeds to unpack its central ideas in an accessible manner, using examples not so much from films or short stories but from aspects of everyday life like the experience of being loved, canned laughter on television, different toilet designs.

The first section takes two paragraphs from *Ecrits* (2001) and uses them for an account of how the symbolic order brings about social links through collective practices and, given the inherent reflexivity in communication, how the gap between the subject of the enunciation and the subject of the enunciated allows us to read unstated meanings in certain utterances. The next two sections explore the ways in which we allow the big Other to believe for us or to enjoy on our behalf and this leads to the enigma of desire: we desire through the Other which means the Other desires through us, but knowing what the Other wants from us is not obvious. Part of the enigma is the unfathomable otherness of another person, the sense that we can never get to the bottom of someone else's personality, the being of their *jouissance*, and the core of this mystery resides in desire. Through its obligations, laws and conventions, the big Other negotiates co-existence with the Other but in the field of sexuality, the most intense and intimate level of intersubjectivity, fantasy is necessary to screen the encounter with the Other and there is a succinct account of this topic in *How To Read Lacan* (pp. 49–60). In section four of the book there is also a good account of 'little object a' using *Richard II* and a more general treatment of the Real.

IN DEFENSE OF LOST CAUSES (2008)

In this book, the most substantial of his politically focused publications that began to be published in 2008, Žižek explores the ideology of liberal democracy, taking up the concerns of the last section of *The Parallax View* and developing what is involved in living in an age where we are supposed to no longer need a Master Signifier to suture the contingent and provide a semblance of a stable whole. What certainly remains is the call of the superego, 'the imperative of *jouissance*' (p. 30), to enjoy and the big Other, not in the traditional form of a hierarchy but in social rules that allow us to live hedonistically, maintaining boundaries between us and the Other, while solidifying the bonds that inhibit solidarity. This is the big Other which, in an age of cherished beliefs in civilized modernity, accepts the legitimacy of discussing whether torture is justifiable. A polemical contrast is drawn between films such as *Titanic*, *Reds*, *Deep Impact* and *The Lives of Others*, where serious historical moments become the backdrop for the playing out of family and personal dramas, and Snyder's *300* where content, the Bolshevik-like discipline of the Spartans at the battle of Thermopylae, and form, the mixing of cinematic digitalization with the genre of the comic book, work together to constitute the film's ideological strength.

Pursuing the question of what is involved in revolutionary change, the legacy of revolutionary justice, from the Jacobins to Lenin and Mao, is not something to be ashamed of but confronted. Accepting the bloody nature of this legacy, Žižek provocatively takes up the term 'divine violence' from Benjamin and uses it alongside the Latin phrase *fiat iustitia pereat mundus* (let there be justice, though the world perish): 'with no cover from the big Other ... [it is] the point of non-distinction between justice and vengeance' when the dispossessed 'imposes its terror' (p. 162). Terror has to be reclaimed and Robespierre repeated and redeemed, without committing the same mistakes, facing down all those from the left and the right who reject such radicalism and dismiss it as dangerous authoritarianism. The kind of revolutionary violence that is today so readily labelled terrorist, the sort of violence that came to the fore under the Jacobins, is read by Žižek as an admission of failure, an hysterical and frustrated response that comes from not being able to properly dismantle the existing order. The terror that Žižek is calling for is exemplified by someone like John Brown and the unconditional nature of his anti-slavery stance; terror is the resolve to change the way we live, 'imposing a new order on quotidian reality' (p. 175).

There is a lengthy account of Mao and his failure to let the Cultural Revolution takes it course by putting the brakes on just at the point where revolutionary forces were entering a new dynamic, with the million-strong Shanghai Commune calling for an anarchist reformation of Chinese society. This account is followed by an analysis of the failure of Stalinism while another chapter begins with a discussion of populism, responds to criticism of the Act and the Real in the book *The Lacanian Left* by Yannis Stravrakakis, and ends by evoking Yeats' lines from 'The Second Coming' ('The best lack all conviction, while the worst / Are full of passionate intensity').

The last section of the book tackles the vexed question of how best to confront the ruling power of capitalism and the state. Žižek firmly rejects the strategy that resorts to a notion of 'subtraction' from the state, by engaging in local struggles where limited resistance is possible, seeing this as an acceptance of capitalism as the unalterable background. 'The point is that there are subtractions and subtractions' (p. 409) and what is needed, he argues, is the Hegelian solution of a 'determinate negation' that results in a positive, not destruction but transformation; a resistance that creates an emancipatory space challenging capitalism and, the negation of negation, one that 'undermines the coordinates of the very system from which it subtracts itself' (p. 409). A Hegelian approach looks for those antagonisms and contradictions within an order, in this case capitalism, that could become the genesis of something new and four areas are identified (pp. 421–8): the ecological and biogenetic challenges, intellectual property as a new commons, challenging the sanctity of private property, and new forms of apartheid in the world's mega-slums. To function effectively as a challenge to the forces of privatization that capitalism would visit on them, these areas need to be quilted by the primary opposition between the included and the excluded (the part of no-part), an opposition that can only be satisfactorily resolved by the common ownership of the domains of the environmental, biogenetic and cultural. The name for this resolution is communism.

VIOLENCE (2008)

We readily recognize the kind of physical violence – the crime and terror that fills our television screens – that Žižek calls subjective violence but we usually fail to see the background that gives rise to it. The concern of *Violence* is with two objective features of this background: the violence of language and the systemic violence practised by the capitalist order. This second kind of violence is invisible in some respects but this does not absolve individuals and their way of life from responsibility: 'The exemplary figures of evil today are not ordinary consumers who pollute the environment and live in a violent world of disintegrating social links, but those who, while fully engaged in creating conditions for such universal devastation and pollution, buy their way out of their own activity, living in gated communities, eating organic food, taking holidays in wildlife preserves, and so on' (p. 23). *Violence* often reads as a series of reflections on events that were recent at the time – the Danish caricatures of Muhammad, the aftermath of hurricane Katrina in New Orleans, the torture of prisoners at Abu Ghraib – or more ongoing issues like the well-practised hypocrisies of the Israel/ Palestine situation but, as with the books that come immediately before and after this one, the overriding concern is how best to formulate a meaningful response to the damage, the violence, that is endemic to capitalism – a response that faces up to the complicity of liberal democracy in this violence. Returning to Benjamin's notion of divine violence, which in its 'emancipatory rage' (p. 159) is emphatically differentiated from fundamentalist violence and cannot be reduced to the envy and resentment of the powerless, it cannot be identified by any objective criteria but relies on the perpetrator's subjective assumption of 'the solitude of sovereign decision' (p. 170), as when the dispossessed of the slum favelas in Rio de Janeiro invaded the city's bourgeois neighbourhoods. Divine violence may be a feature of revolution but it is not a prerequisite and the last chapter of *Violence* presents a clear summary of what is being said about the connections between subjective and objective violence. As to what is to be done, Žižek turns again to Bartleby, this time via José Saramago's novel *Seeing* about an electorate who do not vote for any of the political parties in a general election, effectively dissolving the government. It is better to do nothing than participate in a system that preserves the violence of capitalism:

'The truly difficult thing is to step back, to withdraw ... Sometimes, doing nothing is the most violent thing to do' (p. 183).

FIRST AS TRAGEDY, THEN AS FARCE (2009)

First as Tragedy, Then as Farce is a repetition with a difference – the difference being the world financial crisis of 2008 – of *In Defense of Lost Causes*. The first part of the book is concerned with the way ideology works in a supposedly 'post-ideological' world while the second part focuses on why a reformulated communism is the only appropriate solution to the world's most pressing problems. The difference is a new sense of urgency brought about by the global financial crisis: 'the time for liberal-democratic moralistic blackmail is over. Our side no longer has to go on apologizing; while the other side had better start soon' (p. 8).

A concern with the fetishist mode of ideology, as opposed to identifying its symptoms as the return of what it represses, was raised in the 2008 preface to a new edition of *Enjoy Your Symptom!* and Žižek returns to this idea as a way of accounting for the success of the notion that we now live in a non-ideological world, supposedly united by a spirit of multicultural humanism and the means to enjoy a rich inner life. Rejecting this as a falsity and, instead, embracing communism is for Žižek neither a narcissism of the lost cause or a blindness to the horrors of Stalinism. He agrees with Lenin that a revolutionary moment has to be recognized when it arrives and seized upon, a difference now being the pressing need to do so before ecological and biogenetic fault lines in modern capitalism reduce us 'to abstract subjects devoid of all substantial content, dispossessed of our symbolic substance, our genetic base heavily manipulated, vegetating in an unliveable environment' (p. 92). Žižek differentiates this from the familiar apocalypticism it may sound like and scoffs at any naive belief in restoring mother earth's putative natural balance; instead, there is a frank recognition of the creative ways in which the dynamics of capitalism can contain and normalize the irruptions that threaten it. The free market can accommodate itself to liberal democracy or authoritarianism and therefore a new attitude towards the state is called for, not socialist or anarchist in spirit but Leninist and with the discipline and determination to transform the nature of the state. Allying himself with Badiou's commitment to 'eternal' principles – '*egalitarian justice*, disciplinary *terror*, political *voluntarism*, and *trust in the people*' (p. 125) – Žižek confronts the problem of trying to undermine a 'self-revolutionizing' system fuelled by change and disruption. He looks to the Lenin of *The State and Revolution*, a revolutionary use of state power to transform society and the book concludes with a rallying cry for the possibility of communism on the basis of recognizing there is no big Other, no destiny that has to be fulfilled.

THE FRAGILE ABSOLUTE (2000), THE PUPPET AND THE DWARF (2003), THE MONSTROSITY OF CHRIST (2009)

These three books unfold Žižek's project to appropriate the radical theology that is in Christianity – St Paul's urging to be 'not conformed to this world' but, instead, 'transformed by the renewing of your mind' (Rom. 12:2) – and reclaim it from the repressive clutches of the Church. This brave new task begins in the Lacanian territory of *The Fragile Absolute*, distinguishing between seeing the Symbolic as a primordial intervention that upsets the balance of an organic state, the result of which is the transformation of creaturely instincts into the monstrous drive, and viewing imbalance and excess as always there, a natural malfunction, the Real of the inherent inconsistency, the 'deadlock of pure simultaneity' (p. 93) which the Symbolic strives defensively to pacify. Time, the horizon for the structures of our life, is the attempt to grasp eternity through symbolization, excluding it through an act of repression. This allows for a view of Christianity whereby the Incarnation, the mortality of Christ in time, makes eternity possible – salvation and a coming to terms with the Real through Redemption – but Žižek will have none of this and turns for inspiration to St Paul (Romans 7.7) for his insight into how prohibiting desire only maintains it and to St Luke's Gospel (14.26) for an understanding of *agape* as political love, the need to uncouple oneself from the social hierarchy ('If anyone come to me and does not hate his father and mother, his wife and his children, his brothers and sisters – yes, even his own life – he cannot be my disciple'), reject the equilibrium of 'an eye for an eye' and turn instead to a community of outcasts. This is not a Buddhist-like inner contemplative state but active love rooted in a community.

The Puppet and the Dwarf is an important and eminently readable book for the way it both clarifies Žižek's radical theology and makes clear his new understanding of the Real; what makes it a remarkable work is the way it merges the two, suturing theology and philosophy to explore ideas and prescriptions that will be developed in books that come after it.

Two modes of relating to the Real as a void are outlined: positing it as an impossible limit which we can never reach or postulating it as the negative to be tarried with, the death drive to be sublimated; a duality summed up in words that also find their way into *The Parallax View* three years later: 'The Real is *simultaneously* the Thing to which direct access is not possible and the obstacle which prevents this direct access'.[44]

The shift of perspective that is the passage between these two is also evident in the Hegelian move that sees the separation between man and God to be exactly what brings us close to God; in the figure of Christ, and precisely at the moment on the cross when he feels forsaken and loses his faith, God is separated from himself – the gap between man and God is transposed into the term God – and so: 'We are one with God only when God is no longer one with Himself, but abandons Himself, "internalizing" the radical distance which separates us from Him' (p. 91). There is no simple opposition between two terms, in this case God and man, with a movement from one extreme to another producing a higher order, a synthesis, but a radicalization of the first term. With a shift of perspective that sees divinity in humanity, the Resurrection becomes not some longed-for moment in the future but, in the transformation of our life on earth, something that has already happened. Žižek reads passages from St. Paul in this Hegelian fashion and the biblical story of Job is similarly interpreted (pp. 124–7). Job does not accept his fate, he doubts and disbelieves and rejects the rational explanations proffered by the ideologues who visit him, and like Christ his suffering is meaningless. *Aufhebung* is achieved when the institutional Church is cast off and fidelity to the authentic, atheistic experience it embodies, the realization there is absolutely no big Other, is fully acknowledged and kept alive.

The story of Job is returned to in the first of the two essays by Žižek in *The Monstrosity of Christ*, a book whose subtitle, *Paradox or Dialectic?*, clearly signals the kind of theological concerns raised in *The Puppet and the Dwarf*. The plight of Job is seen as parallel to Christ, a case of 'double kenosis' (p. 57) wherein the gap separating man from God is the distance of God from himself and this divine self-alienation is an aspect of the emergence of subjectivity and the dialectic between Substance and Subject. The second essay, 'Dialectical Clarity versus the Misty Ground of Paradox', concludes Žižek's argument with John Milbank (and, along the way, with Eagleton), the theologian whose essays make up the other part of *The Monstrosity of Christ*.

LIVING IN THE END TIMES (2010)

The book's structure is organized around a five-stage breakdown to the process of grief (denial, anger, bargaining, depression, acceptance) arising from global capitalism 'approaching an apocalyptic zero-point' (p. x). And so, for example, the first chapter delineates some of the contradictory and confusing faces of contemporary liberal societies, like an undesirability for the truth and a general 'ideological regression' (p. 61). The range of topics is so promiscuously wide – Congo, Haiti, Erik Satie's music, Radovan Karadži, to name a random few – that the firm architecture shaping *Living in the End Times* inevitably loses its sharp outlines at times and the reader has little choice but to go with the flow and enjoy endless diversions into history, like seeing the Dark Age of the early Middle Ages as laying a necessary foundation for the rational sciences which would come later, and unexpected examples like the comparison of Josef Fritzl with the von Trapp family in *The Sound of Music*. Familiar ideas and issues – the dialectics of temporality, the political love of Christianity, the Neighbour – are given a fresh airing while films new (Cameron's *Avatar*, Apted's *Enigma*, Mangold's *3:10 to Yuma*) and old (*Berkeley Square*, Daves' *3:10 to Yuma*) receive praise or blame as is their due.

The book's theoretical nucleus lies in Žižek's commitment to the mature Marx of *Capital* who, going beyond his earlier work where it is the producing of the means of subsistence that shapes the world and its superstructure, provided the truth of Lukács' *History and Class Consciousness*: that the worker who comes to see himself as a member of the proletariat *makes* the world a different place. Žižek adds the Hegelian ingredient 'that self-consciousness is itself unconscious' (p. 227), meaning that we make ourselves self-determining beings because this is what we always, already are – we make explicit (in 'self-consciousness'), what is implicit ('unconscious') – and this is why the subject *is* the absolute lack of ground, substance is always subjectivized, and Hegel's Spirit is the self-referencing that actualizes itself in the same kind of way that a nation or communism is nothing in itself but what its members take it to be and bring into existence by their subjective, engaged activity.[45]

What has become a characteristic of Žižek's more recent work, responding to a book or article by another writer in order to defend and finesse his own theoretical positions, is continued in *Living in the End Times* so that, for example, a piece by Mosihe Postone spearheads his own construal of Marx, and Catherine Malabou's *Les nouveaux blesses* (The New Wounded) is used to defend Lacan against her notion of a 'cerebral unconscious'. As was the case with Badiou's *Being and Event* in *The Ticklish Subject*, Žižek brings to attention a book that has not yet been published in English.

Living in the End Times concludes with thoughts on what would characterize a communist culture and the 'divine violence' and Bartleby-like suspension of our libidinal subjugation to power that is necessary to bring such a culture into being.

OTHER PUBLICATIONS

Other publications by Žižek that have not been mentioned above include *Welcome to the Desert of the Real*, a response to al-Qaeda's September 11 attack on the United States, and *The Art of the Ridiculous Sublime*, an essay on Lynch's *Lost Highway*. There are also his introductions to writings of Robespierre (*Virtue and Terror*), Trotsky (*Terrorism and Communism*), Mao Zedong (*On Practice and Contradiction*) and, the most substantial of these, Lenin (*Revolution at the Gates*). There are two collections of Žižek's articles: *Interrogating the Real* and *The Universal Exception*. A comprehensive list of Žižek's publications can be found at The European Graduate School's website (http://www.egs.edu/faculty/slavoj-Žižek/bibliography).

There are also books where Žižek is one of the authors or contributors and one of the more important of these is *Contingency, Hegemony, Universality: Contemporary Dialogues on the Left* with Judith Butler and Ernesto Laclau. *Philosophy in the Present* is a short and very readable debate between Badiou and Žižek while *Lenin Reloaded*, edited by Budgen, Kouvelakis and Žižek, has its origins in a conference on Lenin held in Germany in 2006.

Other publications by Žižek that have been referred to are listed in the References and of the countless others many can be freely accessed online. One important source is http://www.lacan.com while articles written by Žižek for newspapers and journals can be accessed at the publication's webpage. The more important ones are 'In These Times' (http://www.inthesetimes.com/site/about/author/70), *London Review of Books* (http://www.lrb.co.uk), *The Guardian* (http:// www.guardian.co.uk), *The New York Times* (http://www.nytimes. com), *The New Statesman* (http://www.newstatesman.com) and the *International Journal of Žižek Studies* (http://Žižekstudies.org/). A useful list of Žižek's articles with links to the relevant webpages can be found at http://www.egs.edu/faculty/slavoj-Žižek/articles.

FILMS

The Reality of the Virtual (2004)

This film, directed by Ben Wright, is a formal presentation by Žižek that begins with a specific topic, that of the virtual real, but gradually and elegantly it spirals outwards to cover a wide range of ideas.

The explanation of the dimension of the virtual by way of the Lacanian triad, the imaginary, symbolic and real, is quite lucid and benefits from cogent examples ranging from the letters James Joyce and Nora wrote to one another (a negative instance of the imaginary virtual) to the way in which parental authority functions best when it remains at the level of a threat, the knowing look from a paternal figure for example, refraining from actualizing itself in explicit action (the symbolic virtual). Introducing the virtual real, Žižek first explains how the elements of the Lacanian triad are interwoven, so that the entire triad is reflected into each of the three terms. Providing examples for each kind, Žižek runs through the imaginary real, where the real is too strong to confront other than at an imaginary level (the Thing of science fiction films), a symbolic real (the formulae of quantum physics which cannot easily be translated into our lived experience), and the real real which is illustrated by a wicked reading of the Austrians in *The Sound of Music* as the fascists and the Nazi overlords as decadent Jews. Back to the virtual dimension, the real virtual is the missing fourth item from Donald Rumsfeld's party piece at a press conference – the 'unknown knowns', the unconscious, that which you don't know you know, controlling you without you being able to control it. Like the shape created by iron filings attracted by a magnetic field, the virtual real does not exist in itself but it is there as a form structuring the parts of a situation. Another example is provided by the trauma of the Wolf Man in Freud's case, with the witnessing of his parent's sexual act not being traumatic when he saw it but becoming so a number of years later when it was resuscitated as a way of accounting for the difficulties, the imbalance, in his infantile notions of sexuality. This imbalance, the antagonism that can rupture the symbolic, is the real real and the trauma that is resuscitated is a virtual real that accounts for the primal antagonism. The figure of the Jew in anti-Semitism is, likewise, the trauma that is held accountable for the imbalance, the lack of harmony, in the social when really the antagonism that is primal is immanent, it belongs to society. Fascism more generally was an attempt to create an alternative modernism that could abolish this inherent antagonism and, today, liberal capitalism aspires to do likewise. The antagonism is the universal and liberal capitalism is one particular attempt to disguise the underlying class struggle; the universal is not a neutral form but a virtual and the antagonism is played out in the particular.

Žižek's conclusion is to see the real as a formal category, the pure difference that always comes first and does not allow for a neutral position. The world seen from a left-wing perspective is not and cannot be the same world that is seen from the right-wing and the primordial, materialist fact is the difference. Žižek's objection to identity politics, as he explains, follows from this because such a politics of tolerance does not confront the underlying antagonism of class struggle but seeks instead to achieve a space where different positions are tolerated. How silly to think of a world where proletarians and bourgeoisie tolerate one another, each side creatively living out their potential; what is needed is the universal truth that emerges from being embedded in an engaged, partial point of view. The hidden underside of tolerance is an intolerance for the other just as today's injunction to enjoy is accompanied by more and more prohibitions; everything is permitted but nothing happens. Žižek's concludes by calling for a new sense of utopia that involves doing what seems impossible, changing the coordinates and affecting the real of history.

Žižek! (2005)

The documentary *Žižek!*, directed by Astra Taylor and lasting less than 75 minutes, is entertaining to watch as it follows Žižek from Argentina to his home in Slovenia, to Columbia University and an American TV talk show where he explains the superego, then to London before back across the ocean to Boston. It starts with an engaging but serious statement of his basic ontology: the universe as a void, its balance disturbed, a 'cosmic catastrophe ... something went wrong ... it's stupid'. There are some nice moments in the film – like Žižek's dismissal of Lacan's vain posturing in an archive clip from French television or a later scene with him lying in a stylishly dire bed while expounding on the modest claims of philosophy – and a reflective account of the inordinate popularity that has made him a guru figure to some while admitting 'my big worry is to be accepted'. A part of being accepted would involve being seen as the omniscient master, the analyst who is supposed to know, when the whole point is to remove the foundations for a belief in the big Other. The witty ending to the film can be read as a firm refusal on his part to become anyone's *objet petit a*.

Astra Taylor's 2008 film, *Examined Life*, features eight, mostly tenured professors at American universities, delivering ten-minute homilies on philosophical matters while walking, rowing or being driven around different public spaces. There is a certain amount of bland, well-honed generalities from some of the participants but some of them do manage to connect with a recognizably real world and Žižek's high-visibility vest-wearing turn in a London rubbish dump is one of these as he raises a questionable presupposition of much ecological thinking, that of nature's inbuilt balance, and the way it risks becoming a new religion, a way of disavowing the nature of the underlying problem.

The Pervert's Guide to the Cinema (2006)

Produced in 2006, directed by Sophie Fiennes, this 150-minute film is a presentation by Žižek of key Freudian and Lacanian ideas using extracts from over films and at the same time a bold and imaginative defence of the cinematic art. The film is divided into three parts, with the first part introducing and explaining how the art of cinema lies in its ability to play safely with otherwise deeply unsettling aspects of human desire, 'the wound in reality'. The second part looks at the role of fantasy, the void at the heart of subjectivity and differences between male and female fantasy. The concluding section of the film draws together what has gone before by demonstrating how directors like Hitchcock, Tarkovsky and Lynch explore ontological questions about the nature of reality and appearance in ways that bring out the kinship between cinema and philosophy. It is this kinship that makes the film so watchable and appealing to more than just cinephiles.

Videos

There is a number of YouTube and other videos featuring Žižek delivering talks and lectures and some of the better ones can be accessed at http://www.lacan.com/thevideos, including a lengthy 2007 talk in New York, 'Ecology: A New Opium of the Masses', that anticipates many of the concerns of *In Defense of Lost Causes*.

FURTHER READING

Žižek

There is a growing number of books about Žižek, most of which presuppose an acquaintance with his writings and are not always suitable for a reader struggling to read Žižek and make their own sense of his work.[1] An exception is Sarah Kay's *Žižek: A Critical Introduction*. It was published three years before *The Parallax View* and Kay is thus not able to take into account its importance in her introduction to Žižek but this only serves to show the value of what she does say and her book still provides a useful and reliable introduction to Žižek's work up to 2002. One of its values is the importance she places on Žižek's endeavour to read Lacan through Hegel. Kay presents Lacan's objections to Hegel before explaining Žižek's recasting of them in the light of the heterodox Hegel that underpins Žižek's oeuvre, highlighting, for instance, how *Geist* (spirit) is not moving ever onwards to a strict teleological rhythm but only emerges in this way through a retrospective positioning that brings necessity out of contingency. This book also provides a clear account of how an object acquires sublimity and becomes *l'object petit a* and bravely takes on the task of deciphering Lacan's and Žižek's accounts of sexual difference. The last two chapters draw out the importance of a philosophical context for reading Žižek and how his social-cultural concerns, like all his theoretical interests, can only be given the significance they deserve when seen as part of his political understanding of the world and a progressive project that insists on the possibility of real change in the face of cynical postmodernism.

Jodi Dean's *Žižek's Politics* takes up where Kay's book ends and offers an accessible introduction to its subject and while most, if not too many, of its examples are clearly aimed at an American audience there are clear accounts of how Žižek sees the superego enjoyment as an important political factor in contemporary capitalism and the workings of nationalism, Stalinism, democracy and fascism. The book does not, however, take up the political force of Žižek's engagement with theology.

Lacan

Sean Homer's *Jacques Lacan* (2005) can be recommended as a succinct but unrushed account of key Lacanian ideas. It is written in a comfortable but knowledgeable style and serves as the best general introduction to Lacan.

Bailly's *Lacan: A Beginner's Guide* (2009), in conjunction with Sean Homer's, will provide the reader with a sound introduction to Lacan. Bailly, a psychiatrist, psychoanalyst and academic, does a good job of explaining Lacan in plain English, and showing how his ideas can help in the understanding of child development and mental health problems. There are no cultural or literary references, the focus being a refreshingly clear and well balanced clinical approach and this is the strength of the book.

A book for readers 'who are students and teachers, producers and consumer's in today's complex world of visual culture' is Levine's *Lacan Reframed* (2008), a guide to Lacan through the world of the visual arts. Pictorial introductions to Lacan worth reading are Darian Leader's and Judy Grove's *Introducing Lacan* (2005) and Philip Hill's and David Leach's *Lacan For Beginners* (1999). There is a useful and up-to-date dictionary of Lacanian terms at http://www.nosubject.com.

German Idealism

German Philosophy: A Very Short Introduction, by Andrew Bowie, outlines the intellectual background and with chapters on Kant and German Idealism (as well as Marx and Heidegger) this book is a useful starting point for readers new to Kant, Schelling and Hegel. There is a number of introductory guides to Hegel but it is debateable how helpful many of them are in understanding Žižek's reading of the philosopher. Stephen Houlgate's *An Introduction to Hegel: Freedom, Truth & History* (2005) is a helpful place to begin and it includes a good guide to further reading as well as a patient introduction to *Science of Logic*. A website worth looking at is: http://www.marxists.org/reference/archive/hegel/help/foreword.pdf

Adrian Johnston's *Žižek's Ontology* (2008) is not for the absolute beginner but it is a lucidly written account of 'the immanent genesis of the transcendent according to which the subject is both generated out of substance and ontogenetically comes to achieve an autonomy with respect to its substantial ground'.[2] The book is divided into three parts, exploring Žižek's engagement with Kant, Schelling and Hegel ('The chain Kant-Schelling-Hegel, knotted together vis-à-vis Lacan himself as this chain's privileged point de caption, is the underlying skeletal structure holding together the entirety of the Žižekian theoretical edifice'[3]), and Johnston is a superb exegete. In the last chapter, he draws out and amplifies the way a concern with death and the finitude of human existence makes up a crucial, though not always explicit, dimension to the work of Lacan and Žižek. Death, our foreclosed finitude, is the temporal negativity which hollows out and haunts our being; and the raw flesh of mortality constitutes an abiding aspect of the Real. Birth and death are 'two holes in the fabric of subjective reality [which] are filled in and covered over by the fantasmatic formation of the unconscious, with the gaze of the cogito-subject itself being precisely what sutures the wounds inflicted upon the skin of lived experience by vital mortality'.[4]

Introductory guides to Hegel's *Phenomenology of Spirit* like Robert Stern's are helpful for the beginner and when it comes to *Science of Logic*, the single most important work by Hegel for an understanding of Žižek, there are two books which can be recommended: Stephen Houlgate's *The Opening of Hegel's Logic* and, especially, David Gray's Carlson's (2007) *A Commentary to Hegel's 'Science of Logic'*.

ENDNOTES

CHAPTER ONE

1 Eagleton (2006).
2 Adorno (1993, p. 123).
3 Žižek, *The Fright of Real Tears* (2001b, p. 183).
4 Ibid., p. 9.
5 Hauser (2009, p. 18).
6 Žižek, *For They Know Not What They Do* (2008b, p. xciv).
7 Žižek, *The Parallax View* (2006c, p. ix).
8 Metzinger (2010, p. 210).
9 Hauser (2009, p. 2).
10 Žižek, *Enjoy Your Symptom!* (2008a, p. 264).
11 Quoted in Brown (2010).
12 'Slavoj Žižek: interview', *The Observer*, 27 June 2010. http://www.guardian.co.uk/culture/2010/jun/27/slavoj-Žižek-living-end-times
13 Žižek and Daly, *Conversations with Žižek* (2004, p. 31).
14 Quoted in Brown (2010).
15 ' "It was my strict rule, my sole ethical principle, to lie consistently: to invent all symptoms, fabricate all dreams," he [Žižek] reports of his treatment. "It was obsessional neurosis in its absolute purest form. Because you never knew how long it would last, I was always prepared for at least two sessions. I have this incredible fear of what I might discover if I really went into analysis. What if I lost my frenetic theoretical desire? What if I turned into a common person?" Eventually, Žižek claims, he had Miller completely taken in by his charade: "Once I knew what aroused his interest, I invented even more complicated scenarios and dreams. One involved the Bette Davis movie *All About Eve*. Miller's daughter is named Eve, so I told him that I had dreamed about going to a movie with Bette Davis in it. I planned every detail so that when I finished he announced grandly, 'This was your revenge against me!' ".' Boynton (1998).
16 JBTZ Trial, http://en.wikipedia.org/wiki/JBTZ-trial
17 http://www.ff.uni-lj.si/oddelki/filo/english/staff/zizeka.htm
18 http://www.guardian.co.uk/lifeandstyle/2008/aug/09/slavoj.zizek?INTCMP=SRCH

CHAPTER TWO

1 Žižek, *For They Know Not What They Do* (2008b, p. 201).
2 Žižek, *The Parallax View* (2006c, p. 121).
3 Žižek, *The Puppet and the Dwarf* (2003, p. 129, emphasis in original).
4 Žižek, *Did Somebody Say Totalitarianism?* (2002b, p. 60).
5 Žižek, *The Sublime Object of Ideology* (1989, p. 157).
6 Žižek, *The Fright of Real Tears* (2001b, p. 60; Žižek, *The Ticklish Subject* (2000c, pp. 369–70).
7 Žižek, *How to Read Lacan* (2006a, p. 34): 'And one has to think of the phallus not as the organ that immediately expresses the vital force of my being, my virility, and so forth but, precisely, as such an insignia, as a mask that I put on in the same way a king or judge puts on his insignia – phallus is an "organ without a body" that I put on, which attached to my body, without ever becoming its "organic part," namely, forever sticking out as its incoherent, excessive supplement' (Žižek, *Organs without Bodies*, 2004d, p. 87).
8 Žižek, *The Plague of Fantasies* (2008c, p. 174).
9 Žižek, *Enjoy Your Symptom!* (2008a, p. 246).
10 Žižek, *For They Know Not What They Do* (2008b, p. 151).
11 Žižek, *Did Somebody Say Totalitariansim?* (2002b, pp. 248–50).
12 ' "So you are saying that human agreement decides what is true and what is false?" – It is what human beings *say* that is true and false; and they agree in the *language* they use. That is not agreement in opinions but in form of life' (Wittgenstein, 1978, para. 241); Žižek, *For They Know Not What They Do* (2008b, pp. 145–56).
13 Žižek, *For They Know Not What They Do* (2008b, pp. lxviii, 152, 153).
14 Žižek, *Enjoy Your Symptom!* (2008a, pp. 169–75).
15 Žižek, *Tarrying with the Negative* (2004c, p. 14).
16 Žižek, *The Sublime Object of Ideology* (1989, p. 174).
17 Žižek *et al.*, *Contingency, Hegemony, Universality* (2000, pp. 119–20, emphasis in original).
18 Žižek, *Living in the End Times* (2010c, p. 313).
19 Žižek, *The Sublime Object of Ideology* (1989, p. 158); Žižek, *Living in the End Times* (2010c, p. 309).
20 Žižek, *Plague of Fantasies* (2008c, p. 181, emphasis in original). On p. 183, apropos of the same point, Žižek quotes Lacan's quip: 'A madman is not only a beggar who thinks he is a king, but also a king who thinks he is a king.'
21 Žižek, *Tarrying with the Negative* (2004c, p. 121, emphasis in original).
22 Lacan (2004, p. 214, emphasis in original).
23 Lacan (2001, p. 318).
24 Žižek (2002b, p. 41, emphasis in original).
25 Lacan (2008, p. 17); Žižek, *The Sublime Object of Ideology* (1989, p. 174); Žižek, *The Parallax View* (2008b, pp. 131, 144); Žižek, *The Ticklish Subject* (2000c, p. 109); Žižek, *The Parallax View* (2006c, p. 61).
26 Žižek, *The Sublime Object of Ideology* (1989, p. 65).
27 Žižek, *Enjoy Your Symptom!* (2008a, p. 56, emphasis in original).

²⁸ Žižek, *Living in the End Times* (2010c, p. 303).
²⁹ Žižek, *Did Somebody Say Totalitarianism?* (2002b, p. 151).
³⁰ Žižek, *The Sublime Object of Ideology* (1989, p. 194, emphasis in original).
³¹ For the difference between true love and the kind of love associated with the *objet petit a* see Žižek, *Organs without Bodies* (2004d, pp. 162–3) and Žižek, *The Fragile Absolute* (2000b, pp. 20–1).
³² Žižek, *Looking Awry* (1992, p. 4).
³³ Žižek, *The Plague of Fantasies* (2008c, p. 58).
³⁴ Žižek, *On Belief* (2001a, pp. 93–4).
³⁵ Žižek, *In Defense of Lost Causes* (2009b, p. 327).
³⁶ Ibid., p. 328 (emphasis in original).
³⁷ Žižek, *The Prallax View* (2006c, pp. 61–3).
³⁸ Žižek, *The Plague of Fantasies* (2008c, p. 268); Žižek, *The Abyss of Freedom* (1997, p. 23); Žižek, *Did Somebody Say Totalitarianism?* (2002b, p. 183); Žižek, *In Defense of Lost Causes* (2009b, p. 55).
³⁹ Žižek, *The Metastases of Enjoyment* (2005c, p. 116); Freud (2006, pp.118–35); Žižek, *On Belief* (2001a, pp. 81–2).
⁴⁰ Žižek, *Looking Awry* (1992, pp. 14–15).
⁴¹ Žižek, *The Puppet and the Dwarf* (2003, pp. 66–7).
⁴² Žižek, *On Belief* (2001a, p. 80).
⁴³ Ibid., p. 82.
⁴⁴ Žižek, *The Puppet and the Dwarf* (2003, p. 79).
⁴⁵ Žižek, *Enjoy Your Symptom!* (2008a, p. 248): 'what if this very notion that delusive reality is a veil concealing the Horror of the unbearable Thing is false, what if the ultimate veil concealing the Real is the very notion of the horrible Thing behind the veil?' (Žižek, *The Puppet and the Dwarf,* 2003, p. 67).
⁴⁶ Žižek, *The Ticklish Subject* (2000c, p. 56).
⁴⁷ Žižek, *The Sublime Object of Ideology* (1989, p. 173).
⁴⁸ Žižek, *Tarrying with the Negative* (2004c, pp. 36–7, emphasis in original).
⁴⁹ Ibid., p. 36 (emphasis in original).
⁵⁰ Žižek, *Sublime Object of Ideology* (1989, pp. 169–71).
⁵¹ Žižek, *The Metastases of Enjoyment* (2005c, p. 30).
⁵² Žižek, *The Puppet and the Dwarf* (2003, p. 70).
⁵³ Žižek, *For They Know Not What They Do* (2008b, p. xvii).
⁵⁴ Žižek, *Looking Awry* (1992, pp. 29–32).
⁵⁵ Žižek, *Living in the End Times* (2010c, p. 72, emphasis in original).
⁵⁶ Žižek and Daly, *Conversations with Žižek* (2004, pp. 69–70).
⁵⁷ Žižek, *Organs without Bodies* (2004d, pp. 102–3).
⁵⁸ Lacan (2008, p. 70); Žižek, *Tarrying with the Negative* (2004c, p. 37).
⁵⁹ Žižek, *The Metastases of Enjoyment* (2005c, p. 95).
⁶⁰ Žižek, *The Parallax View* (2006c, p. 65).
⁶¹ Diski (1998, p. 8).
⁶² Žižek, *For They Know Not What They Do* (2008b, p. 206). The death drive is what, at the end of China Miéville's *Embassytown* (2011), the Ariekei are on the cusp of experiencing.
⁶³ Žižek, *The Abyss of Freedom* (1997, p. 103).

[64] Žižek, *The Pervert's Guide to the Cinema* (2006d, 16.43–26.14.).

[65] Žižek *et al.*, *The Neighbor* (2005, p. 167).

[66] Žižek, *For They Know Not What They Do* (2008b, p. 206).

[67] Žižek and Daly, *Conversations with Žižek* (2004, p. 135).

[68] Žižek, *The Parallax View* (2006c, p. 231).

[69] Žižek, *The Ticklish Subject* (2000c, p. 291, emphasis in original).

[70] Žižek, *The Parallax View* (2006c, p. 188).

[71] Ibid., p. 121.

[72] Žižek, *The Indivisible Remainder* (2007e, p. 93); Žižek, *Living in the End Times* (2010c, p. 304).

[73] Žižek, *The Metastases of Enjoyment* (2005c, pp. 113–15).

[74] Žižek, *The Parallax View* (2006c, pp. 114–18).

[75] Žižek, *The Fright of Real Tears* (2001b, p. 63).

[76] Lacan (2001, p. 351).

[77] Žižek, *The Plague of Fantasies* (2008c, p. 61).

[78] Quoted in Homer (2005, p. 90).

[79] Žižek, *Looking Awry* (1992, pp. 136–7).

[80] 'Freud himself pointed out that the superego feeds on the forces of the id, which it suppresses and from which it acquires its obscene, malevolent, sneering quality – as if the enjoyment of which the subject is deprived were accumulated in the very place from which the superego's prohibition is enunciated'(Žižek, 1992, p. 159).

[81] Žižek, *The Metastases of Enjoyment* (2005c, p. 68).

[82] Žižek, *The Parallax View* (2006c, pp. 189–90).

[83] Žižek, *The Ticklish Subject* (2000c, p. 281).

[84] Žižek, *Looking Awry* (1992, pp. 6–7, emphasis in original).

[85] Žižek, *The Ticklish Subject* (2000c, p. 281).

[86] Žižek, *Tarrying with the Negative* (2004c, p. 48).

[87] Žižek, *How to Read Lacan* (2006a, p. 57); Lacan (2004, pp. 56–60).

[88] Žižek, *How to Read Lacan* (2006a, p. 58); Žižek and Milbank, *The Monstrosity of Christ* (2009, pp. 56–7); Freud (2006), pp. 526–7).

[89] Žižek, *The Art of the Ridiculous Sublime* (2000a, p. 34); Žižek, *The Fragile ABsolute* (2000b, pp. 76–8).

[90] Žižek and Daly, *Conversations with Žižek* (2004), pp. 112–13); Žižek, *Did Somebody Say Totalitarianism?* (2002b, p. 252); Žižek, *The Ticklish Subject* (2000c, pp. 272–3); Žižek, *How to Read Lacan* (2006a, pp. 47–8).

[91] Žižek, *The Plague of Fantasies* (2008c, pp. 83–4) and Žižek, *The Fright of Real Tears* (2001b, p. 169).

[92] Žižek, *Looking Awry* (1992, pp. 83–7); Žižek, *The Pervert's Guide to the Cinema* (2006d, 1.04.07–1.04.13).

[93] Žižek, *Looking Awry* (1992,, p. 110).

[94] Žižek, *On Belief* (2001a, pp. 45–55); Žižek, *Organs without Bodies* (2004d, pp. 123–33).

[95] Žižek, *The Puppet and the Dwarf* (2003, p. 95).

[96] Žižek, *The Abyss of Freedom* (1997, p. 25).

[97] Žižek, *On Belief* (2001a, p. 80).

[99] Žižek, *Looking Awry* (1992, p. 86).

[100] Benjamin writes of the *aura* that is missing from film: 'for the first time

– and this is the effect of film – man has to operate with his whole living person, yet forgoing its aura. For aura is tied to presence; there is no replica of it' (Benjamin, 1992, p. 231).

[101] '... a quality that makes you feel as though you're standing right next to the actor, no matter where you're sitting in the theatre ... It's a kind of libidinal surrender' (Chaikin, 1972, p. 20).

[102] Žižek and Daly, *Converastions with Žižek* (2004, p. 94); Žižek (2004d, pp. 127–8); Žižek (2006c, p. 179).

[103] Žižek, *The Metastases of Enjoyment* (2005c, p. 178).

[104] Žižek, *The Plague of Fantasies* (2008c, pp. 61–8).

[105] Žižek, *Did Somebody Say Totalitarianism?* (2002b, p. 163); Žižek, *How to Read Lacan* (2006a, pp. 8–9).

[106] Žižek *Virtue and Terror* (2007c, p. xiv).

[107] Žižek *et al.*, *The Neighbor*, (2005, p. 187).

[108] Žižek, *The Pervert's Guide to the Cinema* (2006d, 41: 25–42).

[109] Žižek, *Living in the End Times* (2010c, pp. 2–3).

[110] Žižek, *For They Know Not What They Do* (2008b, pp. 199–200); Žižek, *How to Read Lacan* (2006a, p. 43); Žižek, *The Pervert's Guide to the Cinema* (2006d, 17: 23–7): 'we ourselves are the alien'.

[111] Žižek, *Violence* (2008d, p. 48); Žižek, *How to Read Lacan* (2006a, p. 44).

[112] Žižek, *Enjoy Your Symptom!* (2008a, pp. 8–9).

[113] Žižek and Daly, *Converations with Žižek* (2004, pp. 72–3).

[114] Žižek, *Mapping Ideology* (1995, p. 18).

[115] Fisher (2009, pp. 9–12).

[116] Žižek, *The Puppet and the Dwarf* (2003, p. 36); Žižek, *The Indivisible Remainder* (2007e, pp. 200–1).

[117] Žižek, *Violence* (2008d, p. 31).

[118] Žižek, *The Sublime Object of Ideology* (1989, p. 33).

[119] John Lennon, 'Working Class Hero'.

[120] Žižek, *The Parallax View* (2006c, p. 351); Žižek, *The Sublime Object of Ideology* (1989, p. 35); Žižek, *The Ticklish Subject* (2000c, pp. 325–26).

[121] Žižek, *Welcome to the Desert of the Rael!* (2002c, p. 2).

[122] Žižek, *How to Read Lacan* (2006a, p. 27).

[123] Žižek (2010g).

[124] Žižek, *The Plague of Fantasies* (2008c, pp. 26–7).

[125] Žižek and Hanlon (2001, p. 6).

[126] Žižek, *The Art of the Ridiculous Sublime* (2000a, p. 25).

[127] Žižek, *The Ticklish Subject* (2000c, pp. 53–4); Žižek, *Tarrying with the Negative* (2004c, pp. 266–7; the film, *They Live*, is mistakenly referred to here as *Hidden*).

[128] Žižek, *The Sublime Object of Ideology* (1989, pp. 125–7); Žižek, *The Plague of Fantasies* (2008c, p. 97); Žižek, *Did Somebody Say Totalitarianism?* (2002b, pp. 149–50); see also Žižek, *The Puppet and the Dwarf* (2003, p. 41, the acknowledgement that has to be explained is how anti-Semitism predates capitalism.

[129] Lacan (2004, p. 92).

[130] Žižek, *Living in the End Times* (2010c, p. 68); for an explanation (via Hegel) of the reference on page 68 to the Lacanian trope of how 'the

signifier falls into the signified' in the statement 'A Jew is a Jew', see Žižek, *The Metastases of Enjoyment* (2005c, pp. 43–7).
[131] Žižek, *Tarrying with the Negative* (2004c, pp. 202–5).
[132] Žižek, *The Parallax View* (2006c, p. 300).
[133] Žižek, *The Abyss of Freedom* (1997, p. 28).
[134] Žižek, *Living in the End Times* (2010c, pp. 3–4).
[135] Žižek, *The Metastases of Enjoyment* (2005c, pp. 54–7); Žižek, *How to Read Lacan* (2006a, p. 88); Žižek, *The Metastases of Enjoyment* (2008d, p. 148).
[136] Žižek and Daly, *Conversations with Žižek* (2004, pp. 127–8).
[137] Žižek, *The Parallax View* (2006c, p. 370).

CHAPTER THREE

[1] Hegel (1975, p. 58).
[2] Žižek and Daly, *Conversations with Žižek* (2004, p. 97).
[3] Ibid., p. 25.
[4] Kant (2007, B1, p. 41).
[5] Ibid., A12, p. 59.
[6] Žižek, *The Ticklish Subject* (2000c, p. 55) and Žižek, *Plague* (2008c,p. 267).
[7] Kant (2007, B126, p. 126).
[8] Ibid., A79 (emphasis in original, p. 112).
[9] Ibid., B311 (emphasis in original, p. 272).
[10] Žižek, *On Belief* (2001a, p. 160); Žižek, *Tarrying with the Negative* (2004c, pp. 12–15); Žižek, *The Metastases of Enjoyment* (2005c, p. 186).
[11] Kant (2007, A346, p. 331).
[12] Ibid., A112, p. 139; A107, p. 136; A122, p. 145; B155–6, pp. 167–168.
[13] The paradox of viewing the subject in both noumenal and phenomenal terms can be tamed by adopting a philosophically agnostic position. Thus, in a standard guide to Kant, it can be said: 'For Kant, "I" refers to something over and above my representations, but we cannot know if it is to be the subject of representation or a thing in itself'. Gardner (1999, p. 150).
[14] Žižek, *Tarrying with the Negative* (2004c, p. 15).
[15] Ibid., p. 104.
[16] Žižek, *The Ticklish Subject* (2000c, pp. 197–8).
[17] Žižek, *Tarrying with the Negative* (2004c, p. 37).
[18] Fichte (1982, p. 38); '… intellectual intuition has to do with how philosophy characterizes mind's connection to the world. Kant had seen intellectual intuition as the kind of thought characteristic of the deity, which creates the real object by thinking it. This meant that he denied the possibility of such intuition for finite intellects like ours. For Fichte, it is the coincidence in intellectual intuition of the act of thinking with what is thought that overcomes the idea of a gap between mind and world' (Bowie, 2010, p. 40).
[19] Schelling (1988, p. 26).
[20] Žižek, *The Indivisible Remainder* (2007e, pp. 42–6).

21 Žižek, *The Abyss of Freedom* (1997, pp. 17–18).
22 Ibid., p. 38 (emphasis in orginal).
23 Žižek, *The Fright of Real Tears* (2001b, p. 95).
24 Žižek, *The Indivisible Remainder* (2007e, p. 28).
25 Ibid., p. 13 and Žižek, *The Abyss of Freedom* (1997, pp. 14–15).
26 Žižek, *The Indivisible Remainder* (2007e, p. 32).
27 Žižek, *The Metastases of Enjoyment* (2005c, pp. 129–30).
28 Žižek, *The Sublime Objext of Ideology* (1989, pp. 78–9); Žižek, *The Puppet and the Dwarf* (2003, p. 150); Žižek, *How To Read Lacan* (2006a, p. 63).
29 Žižek, *The Indivisible Remainder* (2007e, pp. 53–4).
30 Žižek and Daly (2004, p. 59). Existentialism suggests that we can touch this primordial abyss of pure freedom when we sense the groundlessness of it all and make a choice.
31 Žižek (1992, p. 69, emphasis in original).
32 Žižek (2008b, p. 129); the same kind of paradox is seen at work in Freudian thought in Žižek, *The Metastases of Enjoyment* (2005c, pp. 30–3).
33 Žižek, *Did Somebody Say Totalitarianism?* (2002b, pp. 174–5).
34 Žižek et al., *Contingency* (2000, p. 227).
35 Beiser ([2006, p. 159); Wood (1990, pp. 3–4); Carlson (2007, p. 23).
36 'For Hegel, totalizations-in-One always fails, the One is always already in excess with regard to itself, it is itself the subversion of what it purports to achieve; and it is this tension internal to the One, the Twoness, which makes the One One and simultaneously dislocates it, it is this tension which is the movement of the "dialectical process". In other words, Hegel effectively denies that there is no Real external to the network of notional representations.' Žižek et al. (2011, p. x).
37 Žižek, *Violence* (2008d, pp. 54–5).
38 Žižek, *The Universal Exception* (2007g, p. xxviii).
39 Žižek, *The Sublime Object of Ideology* (1989, pp. 62–4).
40 Žižek, *For They Know Not What They Do* (2008b, p. 144).
41 Ibid., p. xxvi.
42 Žižek, *Tarrying with the Negative* (2004c, p. 119, emphasis in original).
43 Žižek, *For They Know Not What They Do* (2008b, p. 144).
44 Žižek, *The Parallax View* (2006c, p. 27).
45 Žižek, *The Sublime Object of Desire* (1989, p. 144).
46 Ibid., pp. 175–6.
47 Hegel (1977, p. 383ff. (632ff.)).
48 Žižek, *The Ticklish Subject* (2000c, p. 77).
49 Žižek, *The Metastases of Enjoyment* (2005c, p. 188).
50 Žižek, *Tarrying with the Negative* (2004c, p. 21).
51 Žižek, *The Ticklish Subject* (2000c, pp. 29–30); Žižek, *Enjoy Your Symptom!* (2008a, p. 58); Žižek, *The Metastases of Enjoyment* (2005c p. 145).
52 Žižek, *Enjoy Your Symptom!* (2008a, p. 58, emphasis in original).
53 Hegel [1977], p. 19 (32).
54 Ibid., pp. 18–19 (32).
55 Žižek, *Enjoy Your Symptom!* (2008a, p. 59).

[56] Žižek and Daly, *Conversations with Žižek* (2004, pp. 64–5).
[57] Hegel (1977, p. 19 [32]).
[58] Žižek, *Enjoy Your Symptom!* (2008a, p. 30).
[59] Hegel (1977, pp. 60–1 [98]).
[60] Hegel (1977, p.61 [101], emphasis in original).
[61] Žižek, *The Sublime Object of Ideology* (1989, p. 210); Žižek, *Enjoy Your Symptom!* (2008a, p. 62).
[62] Žižek, *For They Know Not What They Do* (2008b, p. 100, emphasis in original).
[63] Rée (2000).
[64] Žižek, *Organs without Bodies* (2004d, p. 44).
[65] Žižek, *Tarrying with the Negative* (2004c, p. 20).
[66] Hegel (2010, p. 106); Hegel (1969, p. 134): 'First, much is commonly made of the restrictions of thought, of reason, and so forth, and the claim is made that it is impossible to transcend such restrictions. What is lost track of in this claim is that something is already transcended by the very fact of being determined as a restriction. For a determinateness, a limit, is determined as restriction only in opposition to its other in general, that is, in opposition to that which is without its restriction; the other of a restriction is precisely the beyond with respect to it.' The same point is made by Wittgenstein: 'for in order to be able to draw a limit to thought, we should have to find both sides of the limit thinkable (i.e. we should have to be able to think what cannot be thought)' Wittgenstein (1978, p. 3).
[67] Žižek, *The Pervert's Guide to the Cinema* (2006d, 03.21–04.34).
[68] Hegel (1977, p. 89 [147], emphasis in original).
[69] Žižek, *The Parallax View* (2006c, p. 106, emphasis in original).
[70] Žižek, *For They Know Not What They Do* (2008b, p. 58).
[71] A. Rosmini-Serbati, quoted in Boundas (2007, p. 375).
[72] Žižek, *The Ticklish Subject* (2000c, pp. 34–41); Žižek, *The Sublime Object of Ideology* (1989, p. 5).
[73] Žižek and Daly, *Converations with Žižek* (2004, p. 61).
[74] Žižek, *The Ticklish Subject* (2000c, p. 36).
[75] Žižek, *The Parallax View* (2006c, pp. 44–5).
[76] Ibid., p. 61.
[77] Žižek, *The Ticklish Subject* (2000c, p. 55).
[78] Žižek, *For They Know Not What They Do* (2008b, p. 99).
[79] Žižek, *The Pervert's Guide to the Cinema* (2006d, 1.34.30-1.36.58).
[80] Žižek, *For They Know Not What They Do* (2008b, p. xcvi, emphasis in original).
[81] Žižek, *The Parallax View* (2006c, p. 28).
[82] Žižek, *The Defense of Lost Causes* (2009b, p. 127).
[83] Žižek, *The Ticklish Subject* (2000c, p. 99).
[84] Žižek, *Organs without Bodies* (2004d, p. 25).
[85] Žižek, *Tarrying with the Negative* (2004c, p. 129).
[86] Žižek, *The Puppet and the Dwarf* (2003, p. 77); Žižek, *The Parallax View* (2006c, p. 26, emphasis in original).
[87] Hegel (1977, p. 208 [343], emphasis in original).
[88] Žižek, *The Sublime Object of Ideology* (1989, p. 207, emphasis in original).

[89] Ibid., p. 209.
[90] Hegel (1977, p. 10 [17], emphasis in original).
[91] Žižek, *For They Know Not What They Do* (2008b, p. 165).
[92] Žižek, *Enjoy Your Symptom!* (2008a, p. 266).
[93] Žižek, *For They Know Not What They Do* (2008b, p. 99).
[94] Žižek, *The Ticklish Subject* (2000, p. 275).
[95] Žižek, *The Indivisible Remainder* (2007e, p. 211); Hawkins and Mlodinow (2010, p. 44).
[96] Holbein's *The Ambassadors*, which Zizek refers to more than once, is interpreted in this way by Lacan: the form of the figure that becomes a skull depends on the spectator's position so that in the painting the distorted skull is the point where the subject becomes part of the object; the object gazes back, taking the subject's presence into account, 'showing us that, as subjects, we are literally called into the picture' (Lacan, 2004, p. 92).
[97] Johnston (2007, p. 241).
[98] Žižek, *The Ticklish Subject* (2000, p. 160, emphasis in original).
[99] Žižek, *The Sublime Object of Ideology* (1989, p. 226).
[100] Quoted in Žižek, *The Metastases of Enjoyment* (2005c, p. 145); Žižek, *The Abyss of Freedom* (1997, p. 9).
[101] Žižek, *The Cogito and the Unconscious* (1998, p. 248); Žižek and Daly, *Conversations with Žižek* (2004, pp. 59–61); Johnston (2008, pp 167–77).
[102] Žižek, *The Ticklish Subject* (2000, p. 86, emphasis in original).
[103] Žižek, *The Metastases of Enjoyment* (2005c, p. 36).
[104] Ibid., p. 36 (emphasis in original).

CHAPTER FOUR

[1] Žižek, *For They Know Not What They Do* (2008b, p. 100, emphasis in original).
[2] Žižek (2010b, p. 94).
[3] Žižek, *The Fragile Absolute* (2000b, pp. 17–19); Žižek, *On Belief* (2001a, pp. 18–19).
[4] Žižek, *The Fragile Absolute* (2000b, pp. 22–3).
[5] Žižek, *On Belief* (2001a, p. 21).
[6] Žižek, *The Parallax View* (2006c, p. 61).
[7] Ibid., p. 266, p. 118; Žižek, *The Fragile Absolute* (2000b, pp. 17–20).
[8] Žižek, *On Belief* (2001a, p. 15, emphasis in original).
[9] Žižek, *The Indivisible Remainder* (2007e, p. 4); Žižek, *The Sublime Object of Ideology* (1989, p. 18); Žižek, *The Fright of Real Tears* (2001b, p. 166). In Marx, for example: 'The less you eat, drink, buy books, go to the theatre, go dancing, go drinking, think, love, theorize, sing, paint, fence, etc., the more you *save* and the greater will become that treasure which neither moths nor maggots can consume – your capital' (Marx, 1975, p. 361, emphasis in original).
[10] Žižek, *The Fragile Absolute* (2000b, pp. 17–20).
[11] Žižek, *For They Know Not What They Do* (2008b, p. xii).
[12] Žižek, *The Parallax View* (2006c, p. 26).

[13] Žižek, *The Metastases of Enjoyment* (2005c, p. 199).
[14] Žižek, *The Sublime Object of Ideology* (1989, pp. 136–141); Benjamin (1992).
[15] Žižek (2005a). The dream waiting to be realized can also take on a spectral quality: 'The alternative history fantasy of what might have happened is not simply an illusion, but functions as a betrayal or haunting of the Real' (Žižek and Daly, *Conversations with Žižek*, 2004, p. 103).
[16] Žižek, *On Belief* (2001a, p. 84).
[17] Ibid., p. 85.
[18] Žižek, *The Ticklish Subject* (2000c, p. 376).
[19] http://www.youtube.com/watch?v=6MVOKesg4wc
[20] Žižek (2010b, p. 94).
[21] Žižek, *Living in the End Times* (2010c, pp. 69–70).
[22] Žižek, *The Ticklish Subject* (2000c, pp. 374–5).
[23] See, for example, the conclusion to Chapter 5 of Sharpe and Boucher [2010] – 'Although it is often difficult to disentangle the provocations from the positions, it seems that Žižek's frustration with the lack of political resistance to contemporary capitalism is leading him to adopt extreme positions that can easily (as they did with Sorel) prepare a political jump from Left to Right, across the bridge made by reactive hostility to liberal parliamentarianism and representative democracy' – or Simon Critchley's review of *Violence* (2008).
[24] Žižek, *The Ticklish Subject* (2000c, p. 51).
[25] Žižek, *In Defense of Lost Cause* (2009b, pp. 329–30).
[26] Žižek et al., *Contingency, Hegemony, Universality* (2000, p. 254).
[27] Žižek, *For They Know Not What They Do* (2008b, pp. 90–1, 106).
[28] Žižek and Hanlon (2001, p. 10).
[29] Žižek, *Did Somebody Say Totalitarianism?* (2002b, pp. 174–5).
[30] Žižek, *The Arat of the Ridiculous Sublime* (2000a, p. 8); Žižek, *The Fragile Absolute* (2000b, pp. 149–56).
[31] Žižek et al., *Contingency, Hegemony, Universality* (2000, p. 254).
[32] Žižek, *The Plague of Fantasies* (2008c, pp. 275–7).
[33] Žižek (2004b); Žižek, *Revolution at the Gates* (2004b); Žižek, *Did Somebody Say Totalitarianism?* (2002b, pp. 113–17); Žižek, *For They Know Not What They Do* (2008b, pp. 189–91).
[34] Žižek, *Welcome to the Desert of the Real!* (2002c, p. 152).
[35] Žižek, *For They Know Not What They Do* (2008b, p. 189).
[36] Žižek, *Living in the End Times* (2010c, pp. 84–8).
[37] Žižek, *The Parallax View* (2006c, p. 75).
[38] Žižek and Daly, *Conversations with Žižek* (2004, pp. 136–7).
[39] Badiou and Žižek (2009).
[40] Žižek, *The Puppet and the Dward* (2003, pp. 134–5).
[41] Žižek, *In Defense of Lost Causes* (2009b, pp. 188–210).
[42] Žižek, *The Metastases of Enjoyment* (2005c, pp. 102–9).
[43] Lacan (2001, p. 358); Žižek, *First as Tragedy, Then as Farce* (2009a, pp. 86–8; Žižek, *In Defense of Lost Causes* (2009b, pp. 7, 361).
[44] Hauser (2009, p. 15).

[45] Žižek, *The Sublime Object of Ideology* (1989, pp. 38–9).
[46] Žižek (2010f, p. 202, emphasis in original).
[47] Žižek (2010d, p. 97).
[48] Žižek and Daly, *Conversations with Žižek* (2004, p. 108); Žižek (2007f); Žižek, *In Defense of Lost Cause* (2009b, pp. 68–71).
[49] Žižek (2010e).
[50] Žižek, *On Belief* (2001a, p. 148).
[51] Žižek, *Did Somebody Say Totalitarianism?* (2002b, p. 53).
[52] Ibid., p. 177.
[53] Eagleton (2009a, 2009b).
[54] Žižek, *On Belief* (2001a, pp. 146–7).
[55] Žižek, *Revolution at the Gates* (2004b, p. 180).
[56] Žižek, *The Puppet and the Dwarf* (2003, pp. 14–15).
[57] Ibid., p. 138.
[58] Ibid., p. 71.
[59] Žižek (2010d, p. 98).
[60] Žižek (2005b).
[61] Žižek (2010a, p. 180).
[62] Žižek and Milbank, *The Monstrosity of Christ* (2009, p. 61).
[63] Ibid., pp. 101, 287.
[64] Quoted in Žižek (2007c, p. xxxix).
[65] Žižek, *Virtue and Terror* (2007c, p. xxvii).
[66] Ibid., pp. xxvi–xxvii.
[67] Rancière (1999, p. 77).
[68] Žižek, *The Parallax View* (2006c, p. 381, emphasis in original).
[69] Žižek, *Virtue and Terror* (2007c, pp. xxiv–xxv).
[70] Žižek, *In Defense of Lost Causes* (2009b, pp. 162–3); Žižek, *Virtue and Terror* (2007c, pp. x–xi).
[71] Žižek, *In Defense of Lost Causes* (2009b, pp. 192–3); Žižek and Milbank, *The Monstrosity of Christ* (2009, pp. 43–52).
[72] Žižek's commentary on the DVD is available on YouTube (http://www.youtube.com/watch?v=pbgrwNP_gYE).
[73] Žižek, *Revolution at the Gates* (2004b, p. 297).
[74] Žižek, *The Parallax View* (2006c, p. 334).
[75] Žižek (2007d, p. 7); Žižek, *Living in the End Times* (2010c, p. 326).
[76] Žižek, *In Defense of Lost Causes* (2009b, p. 428).
[77] Ibid., p. 374.
[78] Žižek, *How to Read Lacan* (2006a, pp. 26-7).
[79] Žižek, *In Defense of Lost Causes* (2009b, p. 69).
[80] 'Whether "decision" or "act", political action is resolutely confined by Žižek to the individual, and the collective project of class consciousness and revolutionary change envisaged by Marxism is outside the frame of his political analysis' (Parker, 2004, p. 97).
[81] Dean (2006, p. 107); Žižek (2006a, 2006b, 2006c, 2006d, p. 101).
[82] Žižek, *Organs without Bodies* (2004d, p. 12, emphasis in original).
[83] Žižek, *Living in the End Times* (2010c, pp. 84–94).

[84] Žižek, *In Defense of Lost Causes* (2009b, p. 141).
[85] Žižek, *Revolution at the Gates* (2004b, pp. 310–12); 2002a.

CHAPTER FIVE

[1] Žižek, *The Sublime Object of Ideology* (1989, p. 21).
[2] Hegel (1977, p. 208 [343], emphasis in original).
[3] Žižek, *The Sublime Object of Ideology* (1989, pp. 213–15).
[4] Žižek, *Looking Awry* (1992, p. 109).
[5] Žižek, *The Fright of Real Tears* (2001b, pp. 33–5).
[6] 'Or – to put it in Lacanese – the subject's gaze is always-already inscribed into the perceived object itself, in the guise of its "blind spot", that which is "in the object more than the object itself," the point from which the object itself returns the gaze' (Žižek, *The Parallax View* (2006c, p. 17)).
[7] Žižek, *Tarrying with the Negative* (2004c, p. 19).
[8] Kant (2007, p, 137, A109, p. 134, A104).
[9] Žižek, *Tarrying with the Narrative* (2004c, p. 36).
[10] Ibid., p. 36.
[11] Ibid., p. 69.
[12] Ibid., p. 78.
[13] Hegel (1979, p. 221).
[14] 'Thus the symbol manifests itself first of all as the murder of the thing, and this death constitutes in the subject the externalization of his desire' Lacan (2001, p. 114).
[15] 'Even if it communicates nothing, the discourse represents the existence of communication; even if it denies the evidence, it affirms that speech constitutes truth; even if it intended to deceive, the discourse speculates on faith in testimony' (Lacan, 2001, p. 48).
[16] Žižek, *Tarrying with the Negative* (2004c, pp. 119–20).
[17] Ibid., p. 154.
[18] Ibid., p. 156.
[19] Ibid.
[20] Eagleton (1997, p. 7).
[21] Žižek, *The Abyss of Freedom* (1997, pp. 37–46).
[22] Žižek (2004a).
[23] Johnston (2008, p. 69).
[24] Žižek, *The Ticklish Subject* (2000c, pp. 18–20).
[25] Ibid., p. 30.
[26] Ibid., p. 33.
[27] Ibid., p. 61.
[28] Ibid., p. 99.
[29] Ibid., p. 103 (emphasis in original).
[30] Ibid., p. 264.
[31] Ibid., p. 367.
[32] Žižek, *The Fright of Real Tears* (2001b, p. 176).
[33] A comparison of these two scenes from the beginning and the end of *Blue* is also to be found in Žižek, *The Fragile Absolute* (2000b, pp. 101–3).

[34] Žižek, *The Parallax View* (2006c, pp. 29–30).

[35] Žižek, *On Belief* (2001a, p. 107).

[36] Ibid., pp. 79–82.

[37] Žižek, *Did Somebody Say Totalitarianism?* (2002b, p. 77).

[38] Žižek, *The Parallax View* (2006c, p. 26, emphasis in original).

[39] Ibid., p. 114.

[40] Ibid., pp. 167–8, 128–9.

[41] Ibid., pp. 241–2.

[42] Ibid., p. 295.

[43] Ibid., p. 384.

[44] Žižek, *The Puppet and the Dwarf* (2003, p. 77); Žižek, *The Parallax View* (2006c, p. 26).

[45] 'the spirit is essentially active; it makes itself into that which it is in itself, into its own deed, its own creation. In this way, it becomes its own object, and has its own existence before it. And it is the same with the spirit of a nation; it is a specific spirit which makes itself into an actual world which now exists objectively in its religion, its ritual, its customs, constitution and political laws, and in the whole range of its institutions, events and deeds. That is its creation – that is this people' (Hegel, 1975, p. 58).

[46] Sharpe (2004); Parker (2004); Butler (2005); Boucher *et al.* (2005); Bowman and Stamp (2007); Vighi and Feldner (2007); Sharpe and Boucher (2010); Taylor (2010); Vighi (2010).

[47] Johnston (2008, p. 229).

[48] Ibid., p. xiv.

[49] Ibid., p.58.

REFERENCES

Adorno, T. (1993) *Hegel: Three Studies*. Cambridge and London: MIT Press.

Badiou. A. (2007) *Being and Event*. London and New York: Continuum.

Badiou, A. and S. Žižek (2009) *Philosophy in the Present*. Translated by P. Thomas and A. Toscano. London: Polity Press.

Bailly, L. (2009) *Lacan: A Beginner's Guide*. Oxford: Oneworld.

Bain, A., C. Bain, S. Baxter and P. Bloomfield (2009) *Lonely Planet's Ultimate Experiences for a Lifetime*. London: Lonely Planet.

Beiser, F. (2006) *Hegel*. Abingdon and New York: Routledge.

Benjamin, W. (1992) *Illuminations*. Translated by H. Zohn. London: Fontana.

Boucher, G., J. Glynos and M. Sharpe (eds) (2005) *Traversing the Fantasy: Critical Responses to Slavoj Žižek*. Aldershot and Burlington: Ashgate.

Boundas, C. V. (ed.). (2007) *The Edinburgh Companion to Twentieth-century Philosophies*. Edinburgh: Edinburgh University Press.

Bowie, A. (2010) *German Philosophy: A Very Short Introduction*. Oxford: Oxford University Press.

Bowman, P. and R. Stamp (eds). (2007) *The Truth of Žižek*. London and New York: Continuum.

Boynton, R. S. (1998) 'Enjoy your Žižek'. *Lingua Franca*, 8(7) (http://linguafranca.mirror.theinfo.org/9810/zizek.html).

Brown, H. (2010) 'Slavoj Žižek: The World's Hippest Philosopher'. *The Telegraph*, 5 June (http://*www.telegraph.co.uk/culture/books/ authorinterviews/7871302/Slavoj-Žižek-the-worlds-hippest-philosopher.html*).

REFERENCES

Budgen, S., S. Kouvelakis and S. Žižek (2007) *Lenin Reloaded*. Durham, NC and London: Duke University Press.

Butler, R. (2005) *Slavoj Žižek: Live Theory*. London and New York: Continuum.

Carlson, D. A. (2007) *A Commentary to Hegel's 'Science of Logic'*. Basingstoke and New York: Palgrave Macmillan.

Chaikin, J. (1972) *The Presence of the Actor*. New York: Theater Communications Group.

Critchely, S. (2007) *Infinitely Demanding*. London and New York: Verso.

—(2008) 'A Dream of Divine Violence'. *The Independent*, 11 January.

Davey, S. (2009) *Unforgettable Places to See Before You Die*. London: BBC Books.

Dean, J. (2006) *Žižek's Politics*. New York and London: Routledge.

Diski, J. (1998) *Skating to Antarctica*. London: Granta.

Eagleton, T. (1997) 'Enjoy!' *London Review of Books*, 19(23), 7–9.

—(2006) 'On the Contrary: Terry Eagleton on Slavoj Žižek's *The Parallax View*'. *Artforum International*, 22 June.

—(2009a) *Reason, Faith, and Revolution*. New Haven, CT and London: Yale University Press.

—(2009b) *Trouble with Strangers*. Oxford: Wiley-Blackwell.

Fichte, J. G. (1982) *The Science of Knowledge*. Translated by P. Heath and J. Lachs. Cambridge: Cambridge University Press.

Fisher, M. (2009) *Capitalist Realism*. Winchester: O Books.

Freud, S. (2000) *Beyond the Pleasure Principle and other Writings*. London: Penguin.

—(2000) *Interpreting Dreams*. London: Penguin.

Gardner, S. (1999) *Kant and the Critique of Pure Reason*. London: Routledge.

Hauser, M. (2009) 'Humanism is not Enough. An Interview with Slavoj Žižek'. *International Journal of Žižek Studies*, 3(3), pp. 1–20.

Hawkins, S. and L. Mlodinow (2010) *The Grand Design*. London: Bantam Press.

Hegel, G. W. F. (1969) *Science of Logic*. Translated by A.V. Miller. Amherst, MA: Humanity Books.

—(1975) *Lectures on the Philosophy of World History*. Translated by H. B. Nisbet. Cambridge: Cambridge University Press.

—(1977) *Phenomenology of Spirit*. Translated by A. V. Miller. Oxford: Oxford University Press.

REFERENCES

—(1979) *System of Ethical Life and First Philosophy of Spirit.* Translated by H. S. Harris and T. M. Knox. Albany, NY: State University of New York Press.

—(2010) *The Science of Logic.* Translated by G. Di Giovanni. Cambridge: Cambridge University Press.

Heidegger, M. (1985) *Being and Time.* Oxford: Basil Blackwell.

Heinlein, R. A. (1966) *The Unpleasant Profession of Jonathan Hoag.* London: Penguin.

Hill, P. and D. Leach (1999) *Lacan for Beginners.* Hanover: Steerforth Press.

Homer, S. (2005) *Jacques Lacan.* Abingdon and New York: Routledge.

Houlgate, S. (2006) *The Opening of Hegel's Logic.* West Lafayette, IN: Purdue University Press.

—(2005) *An Introduction to Hegel: Freedom, Truth & History.* Malden, MA and Oxford: Blackwell Publishing.

Johnston, A. (2008) *Žižek's Ontology.* Evanston, IL: Northwestern University Press.

Kant, E. (2007) *Critique of Pure Reason.* Basingstoke and New York: Palgrave Macmillan.

Kay, S. (2003) *Žižek: A Critical Introduction.* Cambridge and Maldon: Polity Press.

Lacan, J. (2001) *Écrits: A Selection.* Translated by Alan Sheridan. Abingdon: Routledge.

—(2004) *The Four Fundamental Concepts of Psycho-analysis.* Translated by Alan Sheridan. London: Karnac.

—(2008) *The Ethics of Psychoanalysis.* Translated by Jacques-Alain Miller. Abingdon: Routledge.

Leader, D. and J. Groves (2005) *Introducing Lacan.* London: Icon Books.

Levine, S. Z. (2008) *Lacan Reframed.* London and New York: I.B. Tauris.

Marx, K. (1975) *Early Writings.* Translated by Rodney Livingstone and Gregor Benton. London: Penguin.

Melville, H. (2009) *Billy Budd, Sailor and Selected Tales.* Oxford: Oxford University Press.

Metzinger, T. (2010) *The Ego Tunnel: The Science of the Mind and the Myth of the Self.* New York: Basic Books.

Miéville, C. (2011) *Embassytown.* London: Macmillan

Parker, I. (2004) *Slavoj Žižek: A Critical Introduction.* London and Sterling, VA: Pluto Press.

Rancière, J. (1999) *Dis-agreement: Politics and Philosophy.* Minneapolis, MN: University of Minnesota Press.

Rée, J. (2000) 'Baffled Traveller'. *London Review of Books*, 22 (23), 3–7.

Schelling, F. W. J. (1988) *Ideas for a Philosophy of Nature.* Translated by Andrew Bowie. Cambridge: Cambridge University Press.

Sharpe, M. (2004) *Slavoj Žižek: A Little Piece of the Real.* Aldershot and Burlington: Ashgate.

Sharpe, M. and G. Boucher (eds). (2010) *Žižek and Politics.* Edinburgh: Edinburgh University Press.

Sheckley, R. (1975) *The Robert Sheckley Omnibus.* London: Penguin.

Stern, R. (2002) *Hegel and the Phenomenology of Spirit.* London and New York: Routledge.

Tayor, P. A. (2010) *Žižek and the Media.* Cambridge and Malden, MN: Polity Press.

Vighi, F. (2010) *On Žižek's Dialectics.* London and New York: Continuum.

Vighi, F. and H. Feldner (2007) *Žižek: Beyond Foucault.* Basingstoke and New York: Palgrave Macmillan.

Wittgenstein, L. (1966) *Tractatus Logico-Philosophicus.* Translated by Pears and McGuinness. London: Routledge and Kegan Paul.

—(1978) *Philosophical Investigations.* Oxford: Basil Blackwell.

Wood, A. W. (1990) *Hegel's Ethical Thought.* Cambridge: Cambridge University Press.

Žižek, S. (1989) *The Sublime Object of Ideology.* London and New York: Verso.

—(1992) *Looking Awry.* Cambridge and London: MIT.

—(1995) *Mapping Ideology* London and New York: Verso.

—(1997) *The Abyss of Freedom/Ages of the World.* Ann Arbor, MI: University of Michigan Press.

— (ed), (1998) *Cogito and the Unconscious.* Durham, NH and London: Duke University Press.

—(2000a) *The Art of the Ridiculous Sublime.* Washington, DC: University of Washington Press.

—(2000b) *The Fragile Absolute.* London and New York: Verso.

—(2000c) *The Ticklish Subject.* London and New York: Verso.

—(2001a) *On Belief.* London and New York: Routledge.

REFERENCES

—(2001b) *The Fright of Real Tears: Krzysztof Kieślowski between Theory and Post-theory.* London: British Film Institute.

—(2002a) 'A Plea for Leninist Intolerance'. *Critical Enquiry*, 28 (2), 542–66.

—(2002b) *Did Somebody Say Totalitarianism?* London and New York: Verso.

—(2002c) *Welcome to the Desert of the Real!* London and New York: Verso.

—(2003) *The Puppet and the Dwarf: The Perverse Core of Christianity.* Cambridge and London: MIT Press.

—(2004a) 'Everything you Wanted to Know about Schelling (but Were Afraid to ask Hitchcock)', in A. Welchman and J. Norman (eds), *The New Schelling.* London: Continuum, 30–42.

—(2004b) *Revolution at the Gates.* London and New York: Verso.

—(2004c) *Tarrying with the Negative.* Durham: Duke University Press.

—(2004d) *Organs without Bodies.* New York and London: Routledge

—(2005a) 'Lenin Shot at Finland Station'. *New Left Review*, 27 (16), 23.

—(2005b) 'The Act and its Vicissitudes' (http://www.lacan.com/symptom6_articles/zizek.html).

—(2005c) *The Metastases of Enjoyment.* London and New York: Verso.

—(2006a) *How to Read Lacan.* London: Granta.

—(2006b) *Interrogating the Real.* London and New York: Continuum.

—(2006c) *The Parallax View.* Cambridge, MA: MIT Press.

—(2006d) *The Pervert's Guide to the Cinema*, directed by S. Fiennes. London: P. Guide Ltd.

—(2007a) *On Practice and Contradiction.* London and New York: Verso.

—(2007b) 'Resistance is Surrender'. *London Review of Books*, 29 (22), 7.

—(2007c) 'Robespierre, or, the "Divine Violence" of Terror', in M. Robespierre, *Virtue and Terror.* London and New York: Verso, vii–xxxix.

—(2007d) *Terrorism and Communism.* London and New York: Verso.

—(2007e) *The Indivisible Remainder.* London and New York: Verso.

—(2007f) 'The True Hollywood Left' (http://www.lacan.com/zizhollywood.htm).

REFERENCES

—(2007g) *The Universal Exception.* London and New York: Continuum.

—(2008a) *Enjoy Your Symptom!* (second edn). Abingdon and New York: Routledge.

—(2008b) *For They Know Not What They Do* (second edn). London and New York: Verso.

—(2008c) *The Plague of Fantasies* (second edn). London and New York: Verso.

—(2008d) *Violence.* London: Profile Books.

—(2009a) *First as Tragedy, Then as Farce.* London and New York: Verso.

—(2009b) *In Defense of Lost Causes.* London and New York: Verso.

—(2010a) 'A Meditation on Michelangelo's *Christ on the Cross*', in J. Milbank, S. Žižek and C. Davis (eds), *Paul's New Moment: Continental Philosophy and the Future of Christian Theology.* Grand Rapids, MI: Brazos Press, 169–181.

—(2010b) 'A Permanent Economic Emergency'. *New Left Review,* 64, 85–96.

—(2010c) *Living in the End Times.* London and New York: Verso.

—(2010d) 'Paul and the Truth Event', in J. Milbank, S. Žižek and C. Davis (eds), *Paul's New Moment: Continental Philosophy and the Future of Christian Theology.* Grand Rapids, MI: Brazos Press, pp. 74–99.

—(2010e) 'Soul of the Party: St Paul had it Right – Using Religion to Rock the Foundations of Authority'. *New Statesman,* 1 April.

—(2010f) 'Thinking Backwards: Predestination and Apocalypse', in J. Milbank, S. Žižek, S. and Davis, C. (eds), *Paul's New Moment: Continental Philosophy and the Future of Christian Theology.* Grand Rapids, MI: Brazos Press, 185–210.

—(2010g) 'Can You Give my Son a Job?'. *London Review of Books,* 32 (20), 8.

—(2010h) 'Slavoj Žižek: Interview'. *The Observer,* 27 June (http://www. guardian.co.uk/culture/2010/jun/27/slavoj-zizek-living-end-times).

Žižek, S., J. Butler and E. Laclau (2000) *Contingency, Hegemony, Universality: Contemporary Dialogues on the Left.* London and New York: Verso.

Žižek, S., C. Crockett and C. Davis (eds). (2011) *Hegel and the Infinite.* New York: Columbia University Press.

Žižek, S. and G. Daly (2004) *Conversations with Žižek*. Cambridge and Malden: Polity.

Žižek, S. and C. Hanlon (2001) 'Psychoanalysis and the Post-political: An Interview with Slavoj Žižek'. *New Literary History*, 32 (1), 1–21.

Žižek, S. and J. Milbank (2009) *The Monstrosity of Christ*. Cambridge and London: MIT Press.

Žižek, S., E. Santner and K. Reinhard (2005) *The Neighbor*. Chicago, IL and London: University of Chicago Press.

INDEX

INDEX

INDEX